LITERARY AGENTS

HOW TO GET & WORK WITH THE RIGHT ONE FOR YOU

Michael Larsen

Cincinnati, Ohio

91 90 89 88 87   6 5 4 3 2

Library of Congress Cataloging-in-Publication Data

Larsen, Michael.
    Literary agents.

    Bibliography: p.
    Includes index.
    1. Literary agents. I. Title.
PN163.L37   1986   070.5′2′0922   85-29534
ISBN 0-89879-213-4

This book is dedicated to
the writers it inspires to do their best work
and show an affirming flame,

and to Elizabeth, my divine commission.

CONTENTS

Acknowledgments

Many generous people are entitled to share the credit for this book. The first person who must be thanked is Carol Cartaino, former Editor-in-Chief at Writer's Digest Books, who dared to tempt fate by asking a partner in a small San Francisco literary agency to write the book.

As with *How to Write a Book Proposal*, the staff at Writer's Digest Books—editor Barbara O'Brien, Howard Wells, John Andraud, and Jo Hoff—has been professional, and a pleasure to work with.

To Dominick Abel, Georges Borchardt, Knox Burger, Diane Cleaver, John Cushman, Kris Dahl, Anita Diamant, Sandy Dijkstra, Peter Fleming, Barthold Fles, Joyce Frommer, Russ Galen, Tom Hart, Owen Laster, Ned Leavitt, Scott Meredith, Henry Morrison, Marvin Moss, Gil Parker, Susan Protter, Roberta Pryor, Charlotte Sheedy, Peter Shepherd, Bobbe Siegel, Phil Spitzer, and Al Zuckerman, the agents who took the time to share their wisdom about the business of agenting with me, I am extremely grateful.

For their views from abroad, I would like to thank the following foreign agents: Eliane Benisti, David Grossman, Ib Lauritzen, Ruth Liepman, William Miller, Elfrieda Pexa, and Jonathan Webber.

Special thanks to editors Bob Bender, Liz Hock, and Ann La Farge; author Bill Paxson, Suzanne Juergensen and those agents who read part or all of the manuscript and whose comments have been incorporated into the final version: Marcia Amsterdam, Rick Balkin, Jim and Rosalie Heacock, Perry Knowlton, and Arthur Orrmont.

By going over parts of the manuscript word by word, my agent, Peter Skolnik, improved the book a great deal. His knowledge, authority, and sensitivity inspire both affection and respect.

Thanks go to Bobbe Siegel for permission to use her agency contract and for the friendship so warmly extended by her and her husband Dick. For permission to use the code of ethics of the Independent Literary Agents Association, my thanks to Peter Skolnik and the Association; for using the ethics code of the Society of Authors' Representatives, I am grateful to Perry Knowlton, Carl Brandt, and the SAR.

For joining the index party, thanks to three fine friends and innocent bystanders, Alberta Cooper, Toni Anderson and Bill Cox.

Over the years, many publishing professionals—editors, for the most part—have shared their insights with my partner, Elizabeth Pomada, and me; among them are John Baker, Bob Bender, Cornelia and Mike Bessie, Toni Burbank, Adene Coms, John Dodds, Joyce Engelson, Joe Esposito, Larry Freundlich, Ash Green, Frances Halpern, Pat Holt, Jane

Isay, Betty Jurus, Joe Kanon, Michael Korda, Jim Landis, Dick Marek, Helen Meyer, Brad and Sydny Miner, Luther Nichols, Andy Ross, Jon Segal, and Bob Wyatt. To all of you, named and unnamed, our thanks.

Elizabeth and I would not have gotten as far as we have without the trust and faith of our clients. Thank you for giving us a chance, especially those of you responsible for my "terrific day."

This book evolved in part from the questions of students in our seminars and the participants at the writers' classes, groups, and conferences where we've spoken. For giving us the chance to learn while we teach, thanks to the organizers of these events, especially Jon Kennedy and Steve and Meera Lester at the Writer's Connection; and Paul Lazarus and Mary and Barnaby Conrad of the Santa Barbara Writers' Conference.

Thanks also to author Ron Lichty for allowing me to sit in on one of his excellent seminars on promotion for authors. Some of his ideas found their way into the section on promotion.

Kudos to Al Magary, Epson computer maven, whom I could always call when my QX-10 started acting up. The book wouldn't be as good as it is if my Epson hadn't made the manuscript so easy to revise.

As always, the advice, support, and encouragement of our families—Ray and Maryanne Larsen, Carol Larsen, Rita Pomada, and Sally Ross—have helped to keep us going.

Nothing makes you appreciate how hard it is to write a good book as much as trying to write one. Having to put my knowledge in a book that will be judged by agents, editors, clients, and strangers who make their living reading between the lines made the task onerous.

Yet writing it has given me the chance to repay the agenting and publishing professions for what they have given me. Even more important is what I owe to the authors who got me hooked on books. Short of snuggling with Elizabeth, nothing beats a book I can't tear myself away from, especially if I can read it without the phone ringing!

Elizabeth Pomada got started in publishing and agenting before I did, and she has been with me from day one as agent, author, and partner. Without Elizabeth, I wouldn't have become an agent and this book would not have been written. I hope that, after reading the book, you feel that she chose the right path.

Forewarning

I wrote this book for the best writer and human being you can be. If you write out of what is best in you for what is best in your readers, your work and your life will be blessed with a spiritual dimension that will be your greatest reward. If you can't see the compensation in your bank account, you will feel it when your head hits the pillow.

This book was also written to help you earn the compensation and position in the literary community that your work deserves. The book provides the fastest ways to get the agent, publisher, and deal you want for your book.

The book is directed to writers working on book-length adult fiction and nonfiction. In its tone and approach, it's a very California book. It looks at agents holistically (what could be more California?), in the context of understanding writing, the changing world of books, and your self. Understanding the agenting and publishing process will also help lessen the unavoidable anxieties authors endure.

While writing this book, I tried to imagine that you were one of the many writers we speak to year after year who are intimidated by agents and publishing. I urge you to realize that, as a writer, *you are the most important person in the publishing process*, because you make it go. Except for the unaccountable best seller, there's nothing mysterious about agenting or publishing, only things you may not know yet.

If you're a talented writer, agents and publishers need you more than you need them. You are the reason they exist. Without writers, they'd have to do something else for a living.

Once you know how badly they need you, you can stop worrying about finding an agent and a publisher and do your best work. If you do, you will find both easily.

What you do need is to—
- know who you are and what you want;
- develop your craft;
- have a salable book idea;
- and have a positive but realistic perspective on publishing.

This book will help you meet these needs. Read it, and then act on your knowledge.

The book has seven goals:
- To change your life by changing the way you think about publishing, writing, and perhaps yourself
- To convince you that if you have enough talent and persistence, you will get an agent and your books will be published

- To present the trends and realities of writing, publishing, and agenting that you need to know to get your books published
- To encourage you to create a network with other professionals in the book community, especially writers who share your goals and problems and with whom you may be able to forge enduring personal and professional friendships. Writing may be a lonely calling, but even if you live in the middle of nowhere, it doesn't have to be a solitary enterprise.
- To be an informative, enjoyable, and inspiring reading experience for writers, publishers, and agents
- To be enough of a service to agents that they will say: "This is what I've always wanted to tell my writers."
- To create a dialogue about your needs, problems, questions, suggestions, and experiences that can be used to improve the next edition of this book. I have learned much from writers and want to learn more. If you too would like the next edition to be better, please send me your ideas. Many thanks in advance.

How I Became an Agent

Patty Hearst made me an agent. I had been consulting with Elizabeth Pomada on books she was handling, but when the story of Patty's abduction broke in February 1974, I knew there was a book in it. So I called Tim Findley, one of the two reporters who were collaborating on the page-one stories in the *San Francisco Chronicle*, and asked if he wanted to write a book. He said no, although later he did collaborate on one. I then called the other reporter, Paul Avery, who said maybe.

Fortified with hope, I called Bantam, where I had worked, to see if they wanted to do an instant book on the Symbionese Liberation Army. Bantam was famous for doing instant books, a remarkable public service that they originated. They said no.

Then I called Dell, and the editor there also said no. But, shortly afterward, Helen Meyer, who owned Dell, came in and asked why Dell wasn't doing a book about the SLA, so the editor called back and said yes—and I had just sold a book with four phone calls, an exhilarating experience. Alas, it turned out to be the high point of the whole venture.

The deal was consummated at about the time of the fiery Los Angeles shoot-out that May. We all thought that Patty would soon be captured and that Paul Avery and Vin McLellan, a reporter for the *Boston Phoenix* who came West to coauthor the book, would turn out a quickie to immortalize the meteoric rise and fall of the SLA. Unfortunately, Patty didn't cooperate. She wasn't captured for nineteen months.

When Patty was finally taken in, we held Paul and Vin hostage as they worked day and night in our apartment for two weeks, finishing the manuscript. We had an extra bed in our hallway and alternating typists going around the clock. When the siege was lifted, we toasted the completion of the book with a bottle of SLA leader Cinque's favorite wine, Akadama red, which everyone, including Patty's former fiancé, Steve Weed, signed as a memento of the occasion.

But by that time, half a dozen books had come and gone, and Dell was no longer interested in a quickie. So we resold it as a hardcover, *The Voices of Guns*, and it came out in early 1977, three years after the event that produced it. A hefty hardcover at, in those days, a hefty price, *Voices* weighed in at 544 pages and cost $14.95.

And while *Voices* was then and remains the best book on the SLA, it sank like a stone. It was too much too late, a depressing story the public had already learned more about than it wanted to know in the news media. A TV movie company paid for three option periods, but that too came to naught.

Besides being an exciting introduction to agenting and a book of which we remain very proud, *Voices* was a lesson about the hazards of doing topical books. The situation also presents an unusual example of how far agents are willing to go to help finish a book!

A Hard Year's Night

When writers talk to one another, they may discover that they have had very different experiences with the same agent, editor, or publisher. Every relationship has its own dynamics, depending on the personalities involved, the fate of the book, and the moment, and the relationship will probably change as the project progresses.

This phenomenon is part of the reason why writing this book was the hardest, most intimidating job of my life. It is hazardous to generalize about three endeavors as personal, complex, and varied as writing, publishing, and agenting. No one has a monopoly on truth or virtue. Only the past is certain, and even then, people disagree about it. The only absolute truth is what works for you.

Because books are catalysts for personal and social change, the freedom to write and publish them is essential to our well-being as individuals and as a nation. I wanted every word of this book to sing, because I want it to transform your life. If all it does is to help you appreciate the value of books and the effort that goes into writing, selling, and publishing them, the effort will have been worthwhile.

CHAPTER ONE

What an Agent Does: Before the Sale

DOONESBURY/Garry Trudeau

You may think that it's not important who publishes your first book, as long as it gets published. In that case, you don't need an agent. If your book is good enough, anybody can sell it, because any likely publisher will buy it.

But for your book to become the best book it can be and earn you the most money, it needs four ingredients: the best possible editor, the best possible publisher, the best possible deal, and the right timing.

Editors have their own tastes and publishing houses their own traditions and personalities. They do certain kinds of books better than others. And while there may be more idealism in publishing than in any other business, editors and publishers vary in their abilities and sense of responsibility as much as agents and writers. You cannot surmise a publisher's virtues from its size, its location, or its books.

How can you as a writer get the best possible editor, publisher, and deal for your book? Enter the literary agent.

How An Agent Can Help You

"What publishers do you work for?" This is a question which probably every agent has heard, so the first thing you should know about a literary agent is: Your agent doesn't work for publishers, your agent works for you.

Your agent is a mediator between two realities: you and the marketplace. An agent reads your work and judges its salability. An agent may be able to provide editorial guidance about your idea and your writing that can turn a loser into a winner.

To help a writer, an agent must be a teacher who enjoys explaining what authors need to know about the craft of writing, agenting, and publishing. The lessons start on day one.

When material reaches our doorstep, it arrives in one of four states:

1. Hopeless: Either we don't think it's salable or it's not right for us.
2. The material is hopeless but the writer isn't, and we ask to see the writer's next book.
3. The material has possibilities and we decide with the author how to whip it into publishable condition.
4. The manuscript is perfect and ready to send out.

Number 1 is the case more than 90 percent of the time; number 4, once in a plaid moon. An agent who knows books and publishing can make a world of difference in helping a writer tailor a book to suit publishers' needs. Whether it's a grabbier title, a more marketable angle, a missing ingredient, or smoother prose, by the time an agent sends out a proposal or manuscript, it's usually stronger and more salable than when it arrived.

Why Agents Help Editors

The traditional route to becoming an editor has been through the slush pile. Secretaries would wade through stacks of unsolicited manuscripts, hoping to find a diamond in the rough drafts. If they found one, it might become the first book they got to edit.

When Viking published Judith Guest's best-selling novel *Ordinary People* in the early seventies, it was the first "over-the-transom" book they had published in twenty-six years. Few major publishers now accept unsolicited manuscripts. Before Doubleday stopped reading unsolicited manuscripts, they received 10,000 a year, out of which three or four may have been chosen for publication. Now they and most major publishers rely on agents to scout for and screen manuscripts for them.

With this reliance goes responsibility. Agents put their credibility on the line with every submission. If they submit lemons, editors ignore the fruit and the tree that bore them.

An agent is a marriage broker between a writer and an editor, judging whether a writer and editor will work well together, and whether the writer and the publishing house can live up to each other's expectations. Since agents know the kinds of books different publishers buy, editors' personal tastes, and what they're looking for, they won't waste time sending material that's not right for an editor or a house.

Because they understand the give-and-take of negotiating contracts and the economics of publishing, agents can combine realism and their clients' best interests when making a deal. If they've already sold books to the publisher, they know at what points editors will have room to maneuver on a deal.

Editors work for publishers. Their job is to buy books for as little money as possible and retain as many subsidiary rights as they can for the publisher. This may later poison the relationship between writers and editors and lead writers to switch publishers.

Jim Landis, publisher of Beech Tree Books, his own imprint at William Morrow, once noted: "It is not the business of authors and editors to talk about money." Yet the only way editors can avoid taking advantage of writers is to recommend that they get an agent or a lawyer. Editors know that a bitter fight over a contract will hinder their efforts to concentrate on an author's writing. They also know that being fair to a writer helps foster a permanent relationship.

Editors may not have time to answer all of the questions an author may have or to provide needed hand-holding during the publication process. While they too are always busy, agents work for the writers they represent, so they make the time.

As Bantam editor Toni Burbank put it, working with an agent is like having another doctor on a case who can reinforce an editor's (or an author's) judgment about a project or a situation, or offer a second opinion.

As a knowledgeable buffer between editor and writer, an agent can temper, interpret, and, if warranted, try to alter editorial and publishing decisions. When authors complain, they are nagging. When agents complain, they're doing their job.

Offering the Baby for Adoption

Even some agents recommend that a writer find a publisher for a book, then hunt for an agent, since an agent will be eager to represent a writer whose book is already sold.

Even if your book is so good or commercial that any publisher will buy it, the difference between the best deal and the best editor and worst deal and the worst editor can be as great as that between the right house and the wrong one. But few books are that good or commercial, which means that getting a book to the right editor at the right house for the right price can make the difference between success and failure for the book, and the difference between a friendly, creative, profitable experience and pure hell.

An indifferent editor who's only concerned about the big books or who won't return phone calls can turn the most promising literary enterprise into a nightmare; as can a publisher incapable of producing, distributing, or promoting books or one whose royalty statements can't be trusted. Your book is your baby. The wrong editor or publisher can turn it into a literary miscarriage instead of a source of parental pride.

A writer once came to us ready to quit writing. His first book had been privished (that's the opposite of published) by a small paperback house. He was never able to talk to his editor. He never saw typeset galleys of the manuscript, so he could not respond to the changes that had been made. He only discovered that the book had been published when he found it in a bookstore. He couldn't get his royalties. Finally, the publisher went bankrupt and he couldn't get the rights to the book back.

Your relationship with your editor and publisher is a working marriage, with personal and professional aspects. You have a right to expect them to act competently and responsibly. And since most books are not blockbusters, writers also want publishers and editors with whom they can develop a satisfactory rapport.

We've never met a writer who convinced us that he or she had found the best editor and publisher for a book, let alone made the best deal for it. Over the years, writers have come to us who regretted signing long, intimidating legal documents they didn't understand from publishers they didn't know, but they were so eager to get published that they couldn't resist.

Writers who can place their work successfully are rare. By finding publishers who will buy their books, all they usually do is prove that the projects are salable. An agent who cares will certainly consider the possibility of getting a better editor, publisher, or offer for a book before negotiating a deal that a writer brings in.

Even if you do submit your manuscript yourself and a publisher makes an offer, do not accept the offer if you plan to get an agent to negotiate the deal. You will be tying your agent's hands if you accept a publisher's terms before your agent has the opportunity to better them.

To Market, To Market

When your project is ready to be submitted, your agent discusses with you how best to proceed. Your agent knows which editors and houses to submit your project to and, just as important, which to avoid. Your agent continues to send out your manuscript until it is sold or as long as the agent feels it is salable. Unfortunately, a manuscript may be first-rate but unsalable because publishers feel, perhaps wrongly, that it doesn't fit the needs of the marketplace.

Agents vary in the number of publishers they will submit a manuscript to, depending upon how many publishers they deal with, the feedback they receive from them, how many likely publishers there are for a particular project, how much they like it, and the book's commercial potential.

One agent I know used to submit a manuscript to just four major houses. If none of them took it, he returned the project. Other agents will keep trying for years.

An agent may send out one, two, or three copies of a proposal or manuscript, or as many as thirty copies in a multiple submission.

For a book with strong potential, an agent may conduct an auction, giving publishers a date and ground rules ranging from simple to complex for bidding against one another on a project. With the writer's approval, the agent may simply opt for the house that makes the highest bid or may let editors know that various aspects of the deal, including the editor and the house, will be evaluated in determining the "best offer" for the book.

Rejection as a Way of Life

There's a cartoon in which a writer exults to a friend: "I just got paid for my manuscript. My agent paid me five dollars to take it someplace else." At the Santa Barbara Writers' Conference, a writer once quipped that people become agents for the same reason that they become dentists: They like to inflict pain.

Yet when it comes to enduring rejection, nobody can top literary agents. Rejections are an inevitable part of their daily lives. Nobody collects more rejection slips than agents. It took me three and a half years to sell a client's poster book. My partner, Elizabeth Pomada, collected rejection slips for five years before selling a mystery. But when she finally did sell it, the editor wanted a series.

On the other hand, some books are never sold, despite an agent's best efforts.

Harsh rejections can crush a writer, but agents act as buffers. For them, absorbing turn-downs is just a disagreeable part of the job.

Over the years, we've developed a macabre fascination with rejection. Did you know that:

Zelda wouldn't marry F. Scott Fitzgerald until he sold a story, and he papered his bedroom walls with rejection slips before he won her hand.

Dr. Seuss's first book was rejected two dozen times. The sales of his children's books have soared to one hundred million copies.

Louis L'Amour received 200 rejections before he sold his first word. His books have sold one hundred sixty million copies around the world.

If you visit the "House of Happy Walls," Jack London's beautiful estate in Sonoma County, north of San Franscisco, you will see some of the 600 rejection slips London received before selling his first story. If you want to know how much easier it is to make it as a writer now than it was in London's time, read his wonderful autobiographical novel, *Martin Eden*. Your sufferings will pale compared to what poor Martin endured.

British writer John Creasy received 774 rejections before selling his first story. He then went on to write 564 books, using fourteen names.

Before his first acceptance, William Saroyan accumulated a pile of rejections thirty inches high, perhaps seven thousand in all.

Steve Allen once returned a manuscript sent by a hopeful writer, with the following note: "I thought you'd like to see what some fool is sending out under your name."

Then there is the Chinese rejection notice, which reads:

Honored Sir:

Words cannot express deeply enough the honor you have bestowed upon us in submitting your manuscript. We have read it with boundless delight. It incorporates all the richness and beauty of life and is a triumph of poetic prose. It is our sad duty, however, to have to return your divine composition, and to beg you to forgive our shortsightedness and timidity. We realize that were we to publish this wondrous work, we would immediately be forced to suspend business for we could never again in a thousand years hope to match its immeasurable virtues.

More direct is the response Marcia gets in a Miss Peach cartoon. Three characters are talking, and one says: "Marcia sent her book to a publisher and she got a letter from them!"

"Really?" asks Miss Peach. "What did they say, Marcia?"

"Noncommittal," answers Marcia. "They didn't say yes and they didn't say no. They said: 'Come and take this rotten thing out of here.' Now, a less secure person might take that as a rejection."

This gem is in *Say It Again: Dorothy Uris' Personal Collection of Quotes, Comments and Anecdotes:* "A writer submits a novel to a publisher. After a month goes by without a reply, the writer sends a letter. 'Please report on my manuscript immediately, as I have other irons in the fire,' he wrote. The publisher responds, 'We have considered your manuscript and advise you to put it with the other irons.' "

And finally, there's Snoopy, who has received two of our favorite rejections:

The first is: "Dear Contributor . . . Thank you for submitting your story. We regret that it does not suit our present needs. If it ever does, we're in trouble."

The second reads: "Dear Contributor . . . Thank you for submitting your story to our magazine. To save time we are enclosing two rejection slips: one for this story and one for the next one you send us."

Claws by Claws

When your manuscript is accepted, your agent negotiates the most favorable contract possible for you. The initial negotiation usually covers such matters as the size of the advance and how it will be paid, royalties, how the paperback-reprint income will be divided if the book will first be published as a hard cover, and subsidiary rights the agent wants to retain for you. When you have accepted the offer, your agent asks the editor to send a contract.

For some books, other issues are also important. If your book has best-seller potential, your agent may ask for best-seller escalators, a sum to be paid for each week that the book is on *The New York Times* best-seller list; a first-printing guarantee; or a promotion budget.

When your agent receives the contract, it is reviewed clause by clause. No contract arrives ready to sign. A publisher may have different "standard" boilerplate contracts for agented and unagented authors. If your agent is dealing with a publisher for the first time, the contract review usually leads to one or more long letters or phone calls discussing changes the agent wants in it. If the agent has already sold books to the publisher, he or she knows where the "give" is in the contract, which may speed up the process, and will ask the editor to incorporate previously agreed-upon changes in the contract before mailing it.

Negotiating a contract may take minutes or weeks, depending on the book, the people involved, and the house. Chapter 10 will give you an understanding of the principal clauses in a contract.

The contract for your book is not between your agent and your publisher, so your agent cannot sign it for you. The contract is between you and your publisher. You will be responsible for the literary, financial, and legal obligations it spells out. You must understand, approve, and sign it.

It will contain an agent's clause, enabling your agent to act on your behalf and receive income earned through the contract. The agent deducts a commission, usually 10 or 15 percent, and forwards the balance to you.

This system originated a century ago in England with A.P. Watt, a "wise Scot" whose practices established the literary-agency tradition. (Paul Reynolds, Watt's first American counterpart, began a fifty-two year career in New York in 1892.) A lawyer, Watt used to bill his clients, but they didn't pay him, so he decided to have author's earnings sent directly to him, deduct a 10 percent commission, and then forward the balance to the author.

Publishers prefer this system, because agents protect them from writers claiming they never received what was due them and because agents serve as knowledgeable mediators if questions arise. And as conduits for the money, agents are certain to receive the commissions they have earned.

If you placed your book yourself, you could have a literary lawyer, a rare breed outside of New York, help you negotiate the contract. Lawyers are not usually able to evaluate an editor, publisher, or offer in relation to what better alternatives might be available. That's not their job. What they can do is go over the contract with you to help get you the most favorable terms. Before and after contract negotiations, you're on your own.

But, as the next chapter shows, the signing of the contract is only the end of the beginning. A new world of possibilities has opened for you and your book.

CHAPTER TWO

What an Agent Does: After the Sale

The moment your book is sold, even though it hasn't come out yet, you are no longer just another writer. You are an author! Friends in and out of the literary community accord you a larger measure of respect.

As the publishing process gets under way, your agent continues to serve as a liaison between you and your publisher on editorial, financial, production, and promotional questions. Your agent is with you every step of the way, from the time you start researching the book or working on the manuscript with the editor, to deciding what to do if the book goes out of print.

An infinity of things can go wrong in the publication of a book. Some will. So your agent is also your advocate and a creative problem-solver in trying to resolve difficulties that may arise about revisions, a late, rejected, or undelivered manuscript, your editor's leaving the company, the title, cover design, lack of promotion, or a delayed or faulty royalty statement.

You can read about agency agreements in Chapter 5. Whether or not you have a written agreement, your agent will normally expect to represent all of your work throughout the world in all forms and media.

The exceptions to this include work that is already committed to another agent (having two agents is rare) or buyer, writing you produce as part of your job, and other projects or kinds of writing you and your agent agree to exclude. If, for instance, you write poetry, and your agent doesn't handle it, then you should be free to place it on your own.

Before and often long after publication, your agent pursues the exploitation of all rights to a property. For subsidiary (or sub) rights such as film, foreign, or merchandising rights, your agent may appoint coagents who specialize in these areas.

If your book has strong enough subsidiary-rights potential, your agent may want to start working on those rights before it is sold to a publisher. In fact, if the property is juicy enough, an agent can start whetting buyers' appetites even before having a manuscript to sell.

While agents can solicit interest in or even sell sub rights to a project with a proposal or a finished manuscript, unless a book is very timely or commercial, the logical time to begin is when the manuscript has been accepted and is in its strongest, most salable form. The two areas an agent will want to explore as soon as possible are first-serial sales and the book's movie potential.

Promo Pieces

First-serial sales—getting excerpts into magazines and newspapers before publication—can be both a source of income and an effective way to promote your book.

In general, such sales are more likely for a nonfiction book than a novel from which it may be difficult to cut a strong slice. Obviously, the better known the author or the more timely the idea, the easier it is to sell excerpts from any book.

Local periodicals may buy your work because you're a local writer. National periodicals will only be interested if the subject will appeal to a large audience. But a vast range of specialty magazines—for skiers, car buffs, parents, photographers, you name it—always need material. Although they may not pay much, they will reach the audience for a book on the subject.

Your agent will contact magazines, starting with those boasting the highest circulations and first-serial rates, and offer them one or more article-length excerpts from the book or the right to serialize it.

Hard-cover books arrive in stores about a month before publication, later on the West Coast. The ideal time for an excerpt to run is the month before your book's publication, when books first reach the stores, so that readers who enjoy the excerpt can run right out and buy your book.

A magazine pays more for first-serial sales than for second or post-publication serialization, because the magazine has it exclusively. Different magazines may run different sections of a book concurrently, and the same material may run simultaneously in noncompetitive media.

However, first-serial sales are chancy. Magazines are flooded with material, and editors have been known to take an idea submitted to them and assign it to a staff writer or one with whom they've already worked. They may decide to save money on the excerpt by waiting until after publication. Since many first-serial sales are made for less than a thousand dollars, they generate more publicity than income.

In certain situations, it may make more sense for the author to let the publisher license first-serial rights:

- If the book is heavily illustrated, it may be more practical for the publisher to provide the illustrations to magazines.
- If the book is being rushed to press, there may not be enough time

to sell excerpts, because some magazines have a six-month dead-line. So, given the shortened production time, a publisher may be better able to meet a magazine's tight deadlines.
- The publisher may have a crackerjack first-serial person.
- A book's first-serial potential may not be large enough to warrant an agent's involvement.
- On a big book, a publisher may insist on controlling first-serial rights so it can integrate those sales into its overall marketing plan.

The trade-offs: If your publisher keeps first-serial rights, your share of the income probably will be used to repay the advance. If your agent handles them, your share will be forwarded to you as it's received. Also, although the author usually gets at least 75 percent of a first-serial sale, the split between writer and publisher ranges from 50-50 to 90-10. Your agent only subtracts a commission.

If you are a working journalist with connections to newspaper and magazine editors, you may be able to make your own first-serial sales, and should discuss this possibility with your agent.

The Big Scream

If your book has movie possibilities, your agent will start talking it up to producers, approach a coagent about it, or do both simultaneously.

We once received a funny, imaginative first novel by Ed Davis about a dying old millionairess who hires a swami to transport her soul into the body of her beautiful young nurse who will inherit her money. The swami trips and her soul falls off her penthouse into the body of a drunken bum, leading to humorous complications and a love story with a happy ending. As I was reading the manuscript, it occurred to me that Katherine Hepburn and Lee Marvin would be perfect for the two leading parts.

So at the same time we started sending the manuscript to editors, we also started approaching producers with the project. The first producer to see *Me Two* optioned it. And although we never sold the book—comedies are tough to sell in hard cover or paperback—you can see what Hollywood did with it in the video cassette of the Lily Tomlin-Steve Martin comedy *All of Me*.

While you don't have to use an agent to sell a book, you must have one for TV or movie sales. Producers won't consider unagented material for fear of being sued if they make something similar to a submission they rejected.

Best sellers are occasionally sold in movie auctions for six-figure sums. Most books, however, are optioned for six months or a year. The option period allows a producer time to get a script written. The script is used to interest actors and a director, get financing—perhaps from a studio (or from a network if it's a TV movie)—and make a distribution deal with a major studio if it's to be a feature film.

Nine out of ten options don't get picked up, and even if the one for your book does, a movie is still a long-term proposition. It may take three years or more for a film to go into production and a year to eighteen months more before it's completed and released.

The option price is usually four figures against a five-figure sale price ten times as much—for example, $5,000 against $50,000—if the movie goes into production. Books with strong screen potential will often sell for a five-figure option against a six-figure purchase price; for example, $15,000 against $150,000.

You may get a percentage, usually 2 to 5 percent of the net profits. But between the real expenses of making, distributing, and promoting a film, and the legendarily tricky Hollywood accounting—sometimes the most creative aspect of a production—your 5 percent will be meaningless unless the movie is another *Saturday Night Fever*. If you can't be a "grosser" and get a piece of the gross receipts the movie makes, the purchase price is all you can expect to see.

However, if you're tempted, your agent may be able to get a job for you to write the first draft of the screenplay. This is usually a *pro forma* effort predestined for rejection, so if that happens, don't take it personally. You may also be able to serve as a technical consultant, with screen credit, if your expertise will add to the film's authenticity.

Movie interest in a novel may not develop for decades. Maybe your book will have to wait until you're famous, public interest changes, or the right actor, director, or producer reads it and goes wild for it. It took about three decades for Malcolm Lowry's *Under the Volcano* and Bernard Malamud's *The Natural* to reach the big screen.

From the moment your agent starts trying to sell your book as a movie until audiences determine its fate, movie-making is a very uncertain endeavor. It takes place over a long period of time, and, unless you are a literary superstar, is something over which you will have no control. Time, money, ego, uncertainty, and the craziness movies generate gave rise to the cliché about how a writer should respond to a movie offer: Take the money and run.

While some agents sell their own movie rights, the majority work with one or more coagents, most of whom (along with the studios and producers to whom they sell) are in Hollywood. Literary agents split their normal commissions with their movie agents.

Foreign Rites

When your book is sold, if not before, agents will contact their foreign counterparts to see if there's any interest in the project abroad. Great Britain is usually the most likely target, because of our common cultural heritage and because there are no translation costs. Unfortunately, most books are written in a particular literary and cultural context and don't travel. For instance, most American how-to books on gardening, cooking, sports, and pop psychology won't interest French readers.

Very literary books, such as those of John Updike, and very commercial books, such as those by Judith Krantz, travel, as do books that suit a particular country's tastes and interests. The French and the Japanese love mysteries, and genre romances are popular in many countries. Scandinavians golf in the snow and are eager to learn American techniques, the Japanese are interested in jazz, business, and technology.

Foreign publishers prefer to see most books after they roll off the press. But if a project is timely or strong enough, foreign agents will want to see a completed manuscript or even a proposal. Agents who express early interest in a project will need covers, reviews, bound galleys, finished books, and news of the book's progress.

Sometimes a review in *Publishers Weekly* will spark foreign interest, or a successful launch in America, or just time, may do the trick. Since the United States often takes the lead in introducing new lifestyles and technology, it may take years for foreign interest in a subject to catch up to ours.

Most foreign countries have only a few good local agents, used by out-of-territory agents and publishers to sell their foreign rights. For instance, we have a network of thirteen coagents covering Great Britain and the Commonwealth, France, the German-speaking countries, Italy, Eastern Europe (a great cover for a CIA agent!), Japan, Holland, Scandinavia, Greece, Israel, Turkey, and the Spanish- and Portuguese-speaking countries. American agents usually split a 20 percent commission, sometimes 15 percent in Britain, with their overseas colleagues.

In every country except England, where Charles Dickens had perhaps the first literary agent, the agenting profession is a comparatively new phenomenon. In most countries, authors deal directly with publishers, so agents find books from other countries for their country's publishers and sell their country's books to the United States.

In Japan, France, Italy, and Germany, agents sprang up after World War II, when publishers began to acquire American books. William Miller, an agent in Japan, feels that "the agent working in Japan is not merely acting as a business aid to an author but as a bridge between Japan and the rest of the world over which business can travel." When we sell a book to an English publisher, 40 percent of the sales will often come from

Commonwealth countries outside of England, principally Australia and New Zealand.

As with first-serial sales, if a book has many illustrations, the publisher may be in a better position to coordinate providing different countries with the material they need. The subsidiary- and/or foreign-rights director attends the annual Frankfurt Book Fair, the principal event at which publishers from all over the world buy and sell foreign rights.

The rights director may be able to arrange copublication deals for foreign editions of a book. In a copublication deal, foreign publishers will do run-on editions of a book; that is, print their illustrations as part of the American press run to save on production costs, an important consideration for foreign publishers where picture books are concerned.

Foreign sales tend to be small because of the smaller book and subsidiary-rights markets overseas. Although the advances and royalties for most foreign contracts are smaller than in the United States, you should take heart and remember that books are comparatively just as expensive abroad, often more so than here. Also translators cost publishers money. In Japan, they are so important that their names may be more prominent on book covers than authors' names.

The length of a book changes in translation. A book translated into Hebrew will be shortened by 30 percent; translations into Greek and German will expand it by 20 percent, and a Japanese translation makes it a third longer, perhaps necessitating cuts.

Our English agent, David Grossman, says, "In many ways British publishing practice is far more conservative than in the United States, which is a reflection of a society in which the past usually counts for much more than the present or future." Eliane Benisti in France and Elfrieda Pexa in Italy feel that the same is true for their countries. Nonetheless, as in the United States, big books command big bucks, and while foreign advances don't usually match the American numbers, if your book is sold to half a dozen countries, *mucho dinero* may be heading for your mailbox. And you will also be developing an international audience for your work.

Ruth Liepman, our German agent, speaks for agents in the United States as well as Germany when she observes, "We get a lot of requests from authors, and now and then a top-quality manuscript that makes us all happy. We have not become rich and I do not think we will ever become rich, but we all work hard, read manuscripts and books, look for good terms, and see to it that the publishers pay."

If your publisher keeps foreign rights, it will expect a 25-to-50 percent share of the booty, after deducting the coagents' commissions. This income will be applied against your unearned advance, and what's left will be held until your next royalty period. Your agent simply deducts the commission and forwards the rest to you *tout de suite*.

Oasis

Do words or pictures from your book belong on sheets, T-shirts, coffee mugs, or even toilet paper? If, like Jim Davis's Garfield books, your book sells well enough and has the potential for commercial spin-offs, your agent will investigate merchandising rights.

Your agent keeps an eye out for new rights markets, such as database or software rights or cable TV, which may create possibilities for new subsidiary-rights sales.

Furnishing coagents with what they need, ferrying contracts and other paper work from where they originate to the writers, figuring out exchange rates for various currencies, keeping track of printings and of sales as reported in royalty statements, and preparing tax forms for writers require accuracy, devotion to detail, and time. It simplifies a writer's life to have an agent taking care of these tasks, which generate a steady stream of paper work.

So can litigation. If your book causes a lawsuit, your agent may have to testify on your behalf.

Even after writers die, agents help their estates by continuing to act on behalf of their work on film, foreign, or other rights or reselling out-of-print books if the opportunity arises, and by taking care of royalty payments.

An agent keeps on top of publishing news and trends and what's going on in the world at large that might create opportunities for you. For example, Jay Levinson has written four books about entrepreneuring, an important trend in American business. If I see an article in the paper on the subject that might lend itself to book treatment, I call Jay.

Since your agent is constantly talking with editors, he or she may be able to get you writing assignments. Agents provide editors with lists of available projects or of clients' interests and backgrounds, which editors use to help find a writer for a project. A creative agent may be able to come up with book ideas for you.

An agent may also be able to arrange collaborations between a client and someone with an idea or a story to tell. Celebrity biographies are often collaborations, sometimes unmentioned, between the subject and a professional hired to do the writing.

Your agent can be a first reader for your work and a sounding board for ideas as well as a mentor who helps direct—or if necessary, redirect—your career.

In what may be a desert of rejection, your agent can be an oasis of sympathy and encouragement, a morale booster and confidant who will help you survive the slings and arrows of personal and literary misfortune. It's been said that one of the reasons women are successful as agents is that writers often need mothers as well as agents.

What Agents Can't Do

No matter how skillful they are, there are things agents can't do.

No agent can sell a book nobody will buy. Publishing is a very subjective business. An agent's enthusiasm for a book, however genuine, may be misplaced. And unless it's a hot subject, publishers are reluctant to do "me-too" books that only duplicate what's already on the shelves.

Regardless of how big an author becomes, agents can't devote all of their time to one client. Your agent may be your only agent, but you are not your agent's only client. Agents are continuously trying to juggle their time between all of their clients while responding to an endless stream of letters, meetings, manuscripts, and phone calls. You should communicate with your agent or expect contact only when it's necessary.

However, agents are not mind readers. If you need to talk to your agent, don't wait for a call, make it. Most agents assume that you're busy working away. If you have a serious question or a problem, call or write.

Don't expect an agent to be a publicist, tax expert, savings-and-loan, or to perform personal services for you. One of the joys of the profession, however, is that enduring friendships do develop between writers and agents that can blur the line of responsibility between duty and affection. Mutual dependencies also affect how agents and writers treat each other.

Why an Agent Can Help You

An agent can teach you what you need to know about publishing to ensure your book's success.

By absorbing rejections and being a focal point for your business dealings, your agent helps free you to write.

According to a *Publishers Weekly* poll, editors tend to work their way up the pay scale and the editorial ladder by playing musical chairs: They change jobs every 2.6 years. As a knowledgeable participant in the publishing process and a valuable source of manuscripts, an agent has more clout than a writer, now and at whatever houses editors may migrate to in the future. Since your publisher may change hands and your editor may change jobs at any time, your agent may be the only stable element in your career.

As explained earlier, your share of subsidiary rights will usually be greater if your agent rather than your publisher handles them. And while your publisher will apply your sub-rights income against your advance, your agent will forward it to you as it's received.

For example, on a foreign-rights sale, publishers will keep up to 50 percent of the income. When your agent retains foreign rights for you, only agents' commissions will be deducted, and you will receive all of the balance. It won't help pay back the advance and you won't have to wait until your next royalty statement for it.

Another essential asset for an agent is objectivity. The cliché that a lawyer who represents himself has a fool for a client also applies to writers. When you write a book, you are too close to it to judge its quality or value or speak on its behalf with objectivity; your agent can. (This is why both Elizabeth and I have agents for our books.)

But I have a confession to make: Contrary to any rumors you may have heard, agents are only human. Like writers and publishers, they sometimes misjudge people, books, and situations. They are even capable of adding numbers wrong.

Nonetheless, the selling of your book deserves the same kind of professional care you lavish on your manuscript.

Like publishers, agents—

1. make most of their profit on their big books;
2. should do a good job if they expect to receive a writer's next book;
3. start working with a writer in the hope that they will establish a permanent relationship that will grow more profitable and creative as a writer's career develops.

For most agents, as for publishers, the hardest part of the job is finding good books to sell.

If you are writing to meet the needs of the marketplace, the 1980s may be a golden age for you. A literary agent will make sure you get your share of the gold.

CHAPTER THREE

Six Tips for Finding the Right Agent

Literary agents are a remarkably diverse, independent, individualistic lot. Part of the reason for this is that anybody can agent books. All you need is a desk, office supplies, a telephone, and an address, which explains why many agents, who may think big but start small, work out of their homes.

The small start-up costs, lack of licensing requirements (except for movie agents), deceptive simplicity of the business, and the glamorous aura of publishing attract would-be agents. Consequently, agents vary enormously in their qualifications and operating procedures. Although they all toil at the same job, no two of them do it exactly alike.

Superagent

What are the qualifications for being an agent? Since the relationship between a writer and an agent, like that between a writer and an editor, is a working marriage, the needed personal qualities include the same virtues that help to sustain any marriage: friendliness, honesty, intelligence, toughness, compassion, trust, patience, confidence, initiative, responsiveness, reliability, promptness, courtesy, respect, enthusiasm, chemistry, a sense of humor, loyalty, faith in you and your work, and optimism tinged with fatalism.

On a professional level, an agent needs to have—

The desire and ability to work with all kinds of people
A knowledge and love of writing and books
Creativity in judging books and in helping writers make their work
    more salable
A knowledge of and interest in the publishing business
A knowledge of and credibility with editors and subsidiary-rights
    buyers
A knowledge of contracts and how to negotiate them
An openness to new ideas

Curiosity about anything that could wind up between covers

The ability to judge the quality and value of ideas and manuscripts

The ability to keep track of a changing melange of meetings, phone calls, clients, correspondence, submissions from writers and to editors, deals, projects in different forms and stages, editors and other in-house people, sub-rights contacts, and those in the publishing media

Persistence and creativity in trying to sell a property and in following up during the publication process and after, on sub-rights sales

The recognition that assuming the role of helping to shape a writer's career is a serious responsibility that one must continue to live up to if one expects to keep a client.

Doing It Their Way

Agents vary in their personalities, backgrounds, and in the size and location of their agencies. This leads to a wide spectrum of approaches to running a business. Agents vary in—

How competent they are

How many writers they handle

Whether they accept queries by phone or by mail

How much of a manuscript they'll request at first

How long they take to respond

How involved they get in editing manuscripts and promoting books

How they approach publishers with manuscripts

The number of editors and publishers they deal with

How many publishers they try before giving up on a project

Whether or not they charge fees and how much they are

Their commissions

Whether their agency agreement is oral or written

The terms of their agreements, a subject discussed in Chapter 5

The hours they can be reached

The amount of contact they like with clients.

Agents' tastes, interests, and literary judgements also vary. They also vary in how strongly they have to feel about a project to handle it. Some agents will only represent work they love. Others live by the Hollywood adage: "Sell it, don't smell it."

Some specialize in nonfiction or in literary or commercial fiction. But most can't afford to or don't want to specialize and will consider any adult fiction and nonfiction books for the general public. Some agents will consider young adult and children's books, scripts, poetry, and short work.

Theme and Variations

In seeking an agent, the following six tips will help you find the agent you want:

1. Know your needs. What you need from an agent may be hard to judge, especially if you are looking for your first one. But if you want to avoid being disappointed, figure out the kind of relationship you want with an agent, and then find one whom you think will satisfy your needs.

For example, if you need a lot of personal attention or hand-holding, it would be a mistake to choose an agent who, because of his or her client load or personality, prefers to keep the relationship strictly business.

2. Big or small. Most literary agencies are one- or two-person shops. Medium- and large-size agencies may have half a dozen or more agents, including specialists in movie and foreign rights, first-serial sales, and lawyers who negotiate contracts.

Two large agencies, William Morris and International Creative Management, have offices abroad and in Los Angeles as well as New York. They represent actors, screenwriters, producers, and directors whom they can call on to "package" a movie deal; that is, bring all bankable elements" together to get financing for a movie. These high-powered agencies have overheads to match their clout and are more eager to find commercial properties or those that they can recycle in other media than they are interested in small projects with no sub-rights potential.

That doesn't mean they're not interested in new writers. With an assistant and a secretary, Owen Laster, the head of William Morris's literary department represents over one hundred clients, including James Michener, because he likes to be involved with many projects.

But size alone doesn't make for high-powered agents. Swifty Lazar runs a small agency, but he is a legend in business.

Large agencies have lawyers on staff who review and negotiate contracts, which may save writers a legal fee. While agents in small agencies have to keep a close watch on their clients' financial affairs, large agencies have accounting departments which enables the agents to concentrate on selling. The prestige of being represented by a large agency helps open doors for clients. In large agencies, because different agents handle various rights, the risk of poor communication arises between the writer and these agents who may be on opposite coasts. You can minimize this problem by establishing effective lines of communication with your primary agent, the one who takes you on.

Your goal is to find an agent you will enjoy working with and who will do an effective job for you. Whether you choose to look for a big agency or a small one will depend on you and your assessment of your book.

3. *Reading fees.* Back in the days before paperback auctions, agents' arm-twisting demands, and conglomerate mergers, publishing was a nice, quiet, "gentleman's business." But even today, unobtrusive gentility is still expected of agents in acquiring clients.

Literary agents expect clients to find them through listings in directories, referrals, and their presence at literary events. Advertising, although legal, is frowned upon; so are reading fees.

There are, however, able, responsible agents who charge reading fees and may even edit your manuscript for a fee or a larger commission. *Literary Agents of North America Marketplace* (LANA) notes that 70 percent of the more than eight hundred agents it lists, charge unpublished writers for reading their work. Reading fees are now the norm, not the exception.

However, so-called agents who make most of their incomes reading and editing manuscripts rather than selling them give legitimate fee-charging agents a bad name.

Agents, like editors, reject over 90 percent of what they see. Whether or not they earn a living from agenting, agents may feel entitled to the fee for the time spent reading unsalable material. Some agents refund the fee if they decide to work with the book or when it is sold.

When Elizabeth and I started our agency in 1972, we wanted to see everything. After a year or so, we realized that we had read over one hundred fifty manuscripts and found only two worth handling. To staunch the flow and, we naively hoped, improve the quality of submissions, we decided to charge a twenty-five-dollar fee for reading complete manuscripts (which is what Elizabeth was being paid to review books for the *San Francisco Chronicle*), and to refund the fee if we handled the project. Alas, the jewels—and refunded fees—were few, and finally, we could no longer afford the time.

We don't charge reading fees now, but we start by looking at only the first thirty pages and a synopsis of a completed novel or a proposal for nonfiction. Even that is farther than most editors go when they're wading through the slush pile.

If you're dead set against paying a reading fee, don't. More than one hundred agents don't charge one. But doing so doesn't automatically brand an agent as dishonest. To check if fee-charging agents are reputable, ask what percentage of their income they earn from reading and editing, as opposed to sales of books. The percentage will be greater for a new agent, which doesn't mean the agent isn't reputable.

However, if the agency has been in business for a decade and still derives most of its income from reading and editing, beware. In any case, reassure yourself by asking the agent the qualifying questions listed in the next chapter, which are usually reserved until an agent wants to represent you.

Before sending your work to an agency that charges a reading fee, find out if additional fees are required for editing or reading a revision, whether you will receive a critique of your manuscript, and if and when the agent refunds the fee. Be a wary consumer, as you should be with any new product or service you try, until you're convinced that you are dealing with an experienced, reputable agency.

LANA notes that 50 percent of all agents also require new clients to pay a fee for their costs or services. This charge may be deducted out of the first commission the agent earns. However, one agent asks writers for a 15 percent commission, $100 a month, a *minimum* contribution of $100 for a trip to New York, and to pay for dinners the agent has with editors. The author is also expected to do the initial mailing of the manuscript, at the agent's direction.

There is nothing illegal about this, because agents are free to work any way they want. But the fundamental notion of agenting is that, just as writers risk their time writing a book, agents risk their time selling it. Their basic expenses are supposed to come out of the sales they make, not from their writers.

Risk is one of the most exciting aspects of writing, agenting, and publishing. Books by best-selling authors sometimes fail, while new writers come out of nowhere and build a nest on the best-seller list. Why? Who knows? Maybe your book will be one of the surprises.

4. *A living commission.* A cartoon once portrayed a group of agents sitting around a table, with one of them saying: "We've got to figure out a way to keep these damn writers from getting 90 percent of our income!" Many agents have, by raising their commissions from 10 to 15 percent.

The agenting profession started in England in the 1880s because of the mistreatment of authors by publishers; the growing value and complexity of subsidiary rights in England and America; and the protection of authors' rights provided by the first American copyright law. Mark Twain was one of the first American authors to have an agent. In the United States the number of agents started growing after World War I. (I suppose agents really ought to thank publishers for giving them the opportunity not only to exist but to earn a living by making publishers pay more for books than they would otherwise.) A century ago, an agent's commission was 10 percent, a figure that, with few exceptions, held firm until the 1970s.

This began to change during the recession in the early 1980s. Just as publishers (and everybody else, it seemed) raised their prices, agents started to raise their commissions. Buffeted by rising costs, shrinking advances and royalties, lower bookstore sales, a proliferation of agents, and the greater difficulty of selling books to increasingly cautious publishers, agents were pushed into raising their commissions. *LANA* reports that 47 percent of the agencies it lists now charge 15 percent.

Agents are increasing their commissions out of need, not greed, and are sometimes absorbing costs—such as postage, photocopying, and long-distance telephone calls—previously charged to authors. By the end of the decade, few agents, if any, will *not* be charging 15 percent, at least for new clients.

What you're looking for is an agent who can and wants to provide the representation you need and with whom you will enjoy working. If you find such an agent, wouldn't it be a mistake to let 5 percent of your writing income get in the way of a satisfying relationship?

Agents are free to charge whatever writers are willing to pay them. (Movie agents in California are limited by law to 10 percent.) Agents who provide editorial assistance may charge a commission as high as 25 percent. Agents have talked about starting at 15 percent and going down to 8 percent if sales are high enough. During this transitional period, agents are experimenting to find a fee structure that will be fair to them and their clients. What you accept should seem fair to you.

5. New or used. Agents are springing up around the country. Should you sign up with a new agent or approach those who have been around a while? An agent's stock in trade is his or her contacts and knowledge of writing, books, publishing, contracts, and selling subsidiary rights. An agent can acquire much of this wisdom only through experience.

Nobody grows up wanting to be an agent. The most common traditional path to becoming an agent is by paying one's dues as an editor. An editor is, after all, the in-house agent for a book and, as you will see in Chapter 9, performs many of the same functions. So a new agent who has been an editor of adult fiction and nonfiction at a large trade publisher has a head start in gaining the experience needed for the job. And it was during the recession of the early eighties that many editors who were laid off set up shop as agents. For editors, making the switch from taking advantage of unagented authors to protecting them is an agreeable one.

But publishing experience doesn't guarantee you an effective agent, and the lack of it doesn't preclude someone's becoming an accomplished agent if the person is capable of learning the trade.

The trade-off between established agents and new ones is that, while the former bring experience to the table, new agents may have the eagerness to make a name for themselves, the passion for the project, the time to devote to editing it, and the zeal for selling it that can make up for the difference in experience.

However, unless you have confidence in your agent's ability to negotiate a contract and your agent has negotiated deals the same size as yours, ask him or her to consult with a more experienced agent or a knowledgeable literary lawyer to ensure that the contract will be as finely tuned as possible when it reaches you.

6. The Big Apple syndrome. Two of the biggest nonfiction books of the decade were sold by agents outside New York: Raphael Sagalyn, in Washington, D.C., placed John Naisbitt's *Megatrends*, and Margaret McBride, in Del Mar, California, sold *The One Minute Manager*.

So it's time to demolish a myth about agenting, that an agent has to be in New York. LANA lists agents in forty-eight states and Canada. There are more agents (and publishers) in more places than ever.

But ultimately, agents don't sell books and writers don't sell books. Books sell books. An editor reads a proposal or manuscript and decides either from a literary or commercial point of view, ideally both, that the project is worth publishing. It makes no difference whether the manuscript arrives from across the street or across the country.

One of the reasons that New York is the capital of the world is its unique concentration of radio and television networks, trade and consumer print media, book publishers, the bright, creative people who work for them, and the suppliers who service them, including the financial community, which provides the capital that lubricates this huge engine of commerce.

The heady mix of writers, editors, agents, publishers, packagers, reviewers, trade and consumer media, universities, visitors from all over the world, suppliers including free-lance artists and editors, advertising agencies, and sub-rights markets such as book clubs, newspapers, magazines, syndicates, merchandising companies, and movie, theater, and television producers drives the business onward.

This exhilarating potpourri generates ideas, deals, and an insatiable craving for marketable goods, services, and personalities. Some agents fill their lunch calendars months ahead, others lunch with editors once or twice a week, and still others avoid the ritual altogether, preferring two hours of relative quiet in which to work. But while lunches and parties help keep agents up-to-date on editors' needs and the latest gossip, and deals are certainly consummated over the Dover sole, few agents or editors, if any, make their livings over lunch. They make them by phone and by mail.

During one of our periodic trips to New York, a paperback editor was wining and dining us in a chic midtown bistro. We were delighted when she informed us that she wanted to buy a historical romance series—and then speechless when she didn't want to negotiate the deal! She refused to talk terms over the Beaujolais, and insisted that we wait until she returned to her office and then call her from a phone booth!

Through parties and proximity, New York agents enjoy easier access to the latest gossip; book and magazine editors; article and book assignments; customers for first-serial sales; publicity media; scouts for foreign publishers and visiting editors; and the movie and television buyers based in New York.

So if getting assignments is important to you, you will be better off with a New York agent adept at ferreting them out. However, don't assume that because agents are in The Big Apple they are in the swing of things and see everyone they should.

Over the years, writers around the country have approached us because they were put off by the impression of the New York publishing world as an impenetrable monolith. They had no sense of the perpetual scramble agents and editors endure in search of salable books. Most New York agents are as anxious to find new writers as agents elsewhere, so if you want one in New York, stifle your fears and plunge into the fray.

The Worm in the Apple

Life is a series of trade-offs, and while being an agent in New York makes life easier, as a former native, I can assure you that it also makes life harder.

New York is dirty, dangerous, and expensive. Being mugged or burglarized is not inevitable, but knowing someone who has been is.

The tension that helps create art and commerce also produces a quality of life that is physically and psychologically unhealthy. In New York, anything, good or bad, can happen at any time. This creates an atmosphere of tremendous excitement, but it also exacts its toll on the system. This is what led to the famous cliché: "It's a nice place to visit, but you wouldn't want to live there."

My first boss in publishing was Jerry Baker, the advertising manager at William Morrow, and a very sweet man. A few weeks after I joined the company, in 1967, Jerry retired and took a trip to Greece. Shortly after his return, he had a heart attack and died. He was fifty-eight. A heart attack before sixty is another Big Apple cliché.

Only a few people are important enough to feel that they can make a difference in New York. Everyone else is a tiny cog in an enormous, mindless, nonstop mechanism dedicated to a cherished Knickerbocker tradition: Make a profit any way you can. It takes a great deal of strength to sustain one's personal and professional life in such an environment, which makes the agents and editors who are up to the challenge a hardy lot.

The two tough, relentless, ubiquitous symbols of what it takes to survive and thrive in the Big Apple are the taxicab and the cockroach. As a visitor, the most important distinction to keep in mind about these two creations is that you can always get a cockroach on a rainy day.

New York doesn't start things; it commercializes them. In manufacturing terms, the rest of America is the R&D department; New York is the executive suite. Publishing people go to the same parties, see the same people, read the same media, and live the same life-style. This breeds a provincialism that says: "If we don't know about it, it doesn't exist." Until a trend is sanctified by *Time* or *The New York Times*, it doesn't merit recognition.

Two Points on the Bottom Line

1. Like editors, agents don't go into the business to get rich. They do it because they like books and they like people. Publishing is a people business sustained by profit and personal relationships.

2. Agents don't work for publishers; they work for writers. And when their publishers may be on a distant shore, many writers prefer an agent closer to home. Ability and compatibility are what count most, not geography.

CHAPTER FOUR

Making Connections

If you're thinking about getting an agent, you're in for a pleasant surprise. It's been said that an agent is like a bank loan—you can only get one if you can prove you don't need it. Writers, editors, and agents themselves help perpetuate the greatest myth in publishing: It's hard to get an agent. Nonsense! It's easy to get an agent. What's hard is writing a salable book.

You find an agent the same way an agent finds a publisher: by having something salable to sell and being professional in your approach. Finding an agent is getting easier all the time, because agencies are springing up around the country. As I mentioned in the last chapter, *Literary Agents of North America* lists more than eight hundred agents in forty-eight states and Canada. If you have a marketable book project, the challenge isn't finding an agent. It's finding a competent, reputable agent you feel comfortable working with.

When to Look for an Agent

Unless your short stories or articles consistently command four-figure sums, most agents will be unwilling to handle only them, because their commissions won't justify the time spent placing them. But if an agent is representing you on a book, he or she may be willing to take care of your less profitable work as a courtesy.

The moment you have a proposal with sample chapters for a nonfiction book or a complete manuscript that is 100 percent—as well conceived and crafted as you can make it—agents will be glad to hear from you.

Until you've completed a novel, you can't prove that you can sustain plot and characterization for at least 50,000 words or two hundred pages, so a first novel should usually be finished. Writers often call and ask us to read their first few chapters "to see if I should bother continuing." An agent's job is to sell books, not to read partial manuscripts and offer free advice about whether a writer is on the right track.

Publishers are offered too many completed novels for them to be interested in unfinished fiction by unpublished writers. Although category romances can be sold with three chapters and an outline, this is rare with mainstream novels, unless you have already had others published. However, if you're planning a novel of six hundred pages or more, and you have two hundred smashing pages and an extensive, dynamite outline of the plot and the characters, your book might be an exception.

If you've had articles published or have special expertise on a subject, a proposal with one or two sample chapters will suffice for a nonfiction book.

Where to Look for an Agent

1. *Your professional network.* The moment you were born, you had a personal network: your family. As you grew up, you enlarged your personal network with friends, schoolmates, and coworkers.

You can overcome the isolation of writing by developing a nationwide professional network of writers, editors, booksellers, reviewers, librarians, writing teachers, publicists, publishers' sales representatives, media people, and fans of your work.

You can join local and national writers' organizations. You can become part of a writers' group that meets regularly to critique its members' work. You can attend classes, seminars, and conferences.

If you have a computer and a modem, you can join or start a SIG, a Special Interest Group for writers, so you can communicate with writers around the country.

In addition to the consolation and encouragement they can offer as friends, book people can be valuable sources of advice about agents, publishers, ideas, writing, research, and promotion.

You have both direct and indirect networks. Your direct network is all the people you know; your indirect network is everyone they know. Continue to develop your personal and professional networks throughout your career. They can be powerful allies in your quest for success.

2. *SAR and ILAA.* The Society of Authors' Representatives and the Independent Literary Agents Association are the two agents' organizations; their members are experienced and reputable. The SAR was founded in 1928, and is made up of fifty-two of the generally larger, older agencies. Only New York agents may join. For a helpful brochure and membership list, send a SASE to SAR, 39½ Washington Square South, New York NY 10012.

Formed in the mid-1970s, with Elizabeth and me among the charter members, ILAA has eight-five members, from generally newer, smaller agencies in and out of New York. Send a SASE to ILAA, % Ellen Levine Literary Agency, 432 Park Avenue South, New York NY 10016, for a brochure and membership list.

3. Directories. The directory mentioned earlier, *Literary Agents of North America Marketplace: The Complete Guide to U.S. and Canadian Literary Agencies* is the most complete guide to agents on the market. In addition to describing agents' interests and policies, it lists agencies by size and location. To order *LANA*, contact Author Aid/Research Associates International, 340 East 52nd Street, New York NY 10022, (212)758-4213.

Literary Agents: A Writer's Guide by Debby Mayer, A Poets & Writers Book, contains a listing of agents preceded by an explanation of how agents work and how to find one.

In addition, there's *Literary Market Place* and *Writer's Market,* two annual compendiums listing agents who have sold books. These directories should be in your local library. *Writer's Market* is sold in bookstores.

For agents in your area, try the yellow pages.

4. Literary events. Writing classes, seminars, and conferences present opportunities to meet or learn about agents. Autograph parties, readings, and lectures may also be helpful.

5. Books. Check the acknowledgment page of your favorite books or books related to the one you're writing. Writers occasionally thank their agents in print.

Making the Connection

Regardless of how they operate, agents like to be queried properly, either by phone, or, as is more often the case, by mail. If the agency is small, try calling. However, don't ask to meet the agent, something writers are sometimes anxious to do before their work has been read. Since the prevailing rejection rate is over 90 percent, the chance that the agent will like the work is less than one out of ten, so a meeting will waste both the agent's and writer's time. Agents don't want to meet with new writers until they've read something they want to handle.

If you write to an agent, keep it simple. Prepare a one-page query letter for a nonfiction book. For fiction, prepare a one- or two-page letter including information about yourself, and a synopsis briefly describing the plot and the characters.

Free-lance writers who sell articles with query letters know the importance of making them impeccable. Your letter is a sample of your writing. Spelling or grammatical errors or awkward, flat prose mark you instantly as a bad writer. Regard a query letter as a piece of professional writing, since that's the business the agent is in and the one you are aspiring to join.

Type the query immaculately, and include your address, day and evening phone numbers, and a self-addressed, stamped envelope.

Agents are used to multiple query letters, although we do begin to wonder when we get a query addressed to "Occupant." (Just kidding.) But an individually typed query makes a better impression than an obvious photocopy, especially in the computer age. If it's a multiple query, mention it. In responding to a query, an agent might even suggest a more salable slant for the book. If you plan to submit your manuscript to more than one agent at a time, ask first if it's all right. Many agents can't afford the luxury of reading a manuscript that they may not be able to handle.

The more income agents are earning with their present roster of clients, the less anxious they are to take on new writers and the harder it will be for you to break in. However, 87 percent of the agents listed in LANA read unsolicited queries, as distinguished from unsolicited manuscripts. At large agencies, it will be more likely to be read if it's addressed to a specific individual. But don't expect an answer unless you include a stamped, self-addressed envelope.

How to Submit Your Manuscript

A writer named Karen Elizabeth Rigley once lamented: "Sometimes, it feels like I'm submitting boomerangs instead of manuscripts." To help avoid having agents bounce your work back at you or not return it at all, submit your manuscript properly.

The appearance of your material reflects the professionalism with which you are approaching the agent, the subject, and your career. It's the tangible evidence of the care you have taken with the proposal or manuscript. Consequently, the impression of you it makes will affect readers' reactions to the project. Make your manuscript a document that looks like it's worth the advance you want for it. Agents and editors know from experience that there is usually a relationship between how a manuscript looks and how it reads.

One of our favorite William Hamilton cartoons shows an ambitious-looking young writer confiding to a lady friend, over a glass of wine: "I haven't actually been published or produced yet but I have had some things professionally typed." Whether you do it yourself or have someone else do it, make sure your manuscript is professionally typed.

Type your manuscript immaculately on one side of 8½-by 11-inch twenty-pound bond paper. Never use slippery, erasable onionskin. Type everything, including quotes and anecdotes, double-spaced. Avoid "widows," a subhead at the bottom of a page or the last line of a chapter at the top of one.

Your typewriter should have a standard, serif, pica—10 characters to an inch—typeface, a new ribbon, and clean keys. (Serif faces have cross strokes at the tops and bottoms of letters, which make them more readable.) If you use a word processor, use a letter-quality printer. Don't make the right margin even; that's the typesetter's job. If you have a continuous-sheet printer, use 20-pound paper and separate the pages before mailing the manuscript.

Type twenty-five sixty-character lines, or about two hundred fifty words on a page. Set 1¼-inch margins on the top and sides of the page (1¾ inches if you must use a typewriter with elite type).

At the left margin of each page, half an inch from the top, type your last name/first key word from the title. On the same line, at the right margin, type the number of the page.

"I've got all the pages numbered," bragged the writer ready to conquer the world. "Now all I have to do is fill in the rest." After you fill in the rest, be sure that your pages are numbered consecutively from 1 to the end of the manuscript, not by chapter or the parts of a proposal, so if the manuscript is dropped, it will be easy to reassemble the pages.

Proofread your manuscript carefully and get an eagle-eyed friend to check your work. If you're using a computer, proofread a printout to catch what you may have missed on the screen, especially those extra spaces between words that can creep into your prose.

Submit manuscripts unbound, without staples, paper clips, or any form of binding. Send high-quality photocopies of your text and illustrations, or duplicates of slides. *Always keep a copy of anything you submit.*

If you're sending a proposal, a children's book, or a short sample of the manuscript, you may use a rubber band or paper clip. But for a more professional look and greater protection in case you have to resubmit the material, insert it in the right side of a colored, double-pocket construction-paper portfolio. Type the title and your name on a self-adhesive label and stick it on the cover. Use the left pocket for writing samples or illustrations.

In your covering letter, briefly discuss your life and work and the essence of the book. Try to keep it to one page of single-spaced copy. Type your name, address, and day and evening telephone numbers on the title page and on all correspondence.

If you have a computer, mention the model, the disks, and the word-processing program you use. Your publisher may be able to use your disks to speed up the typesetting process.

In *How to Write Short Stories*, Ring Lardner warns: "A good many young writers make the mistake of enclosing a stamped, self-addressed envelope, big enough for the manuscript to come back in. This is too much of a temptation to the editor." Unfortunately, without a SASE, an agent or editor will probably not return your material.

And, as agents and publishers do not assume responsibility for lost or damaged manuscripts, it behooves you to package your material neatly and carefully. For a short work, use a manila envelope, or, for greater protection, a #5 mailing bag. Enclose another stamped, self-addressed mailer if you want the material returned. Never send loose stamps. If you don't need the material back, say so. But include a stamped, self-addressed #10 envelope if you want a response. Five staples will seal a mailing bag effectively; avoid string or tape, and don't tape letters to the outside of the package.

It shouldn't take an agent longer to open the package than it does to read the manuscript. Unbelievable but true: We once received a manuscript that was wrapped in plastic, put in a box, wrapped in foil, covered in a sheet of plastic bubbles, put in another box with shredded paper, then wrapped again in brown paper and again with wire, and then the edges were taped! A sure-fire candidate for instant incineration!

If you're sending a complete manuscript, insert it in a box, perhaps the box a ream of paper comes in, and use a #6 or #7 mailing bag, depending on the length of the manuscript.

Naturally, you want to be sure your proposal arrives. But *don't call*. Since they may not keep a log of incoming manuscripts, agents dislike wasting their time sifting through piles of submissions to respond to did-you-get-it calls. Use United Parcel Service, spring for a return receipt at the post office, or enclose a postcard with your address filled in and the following message on the back:

We received (Title) on _____ .
We will get back to you by _____ .
Name _____ .

Be sure to send your covering letter and SASE with the manuscript, so an agent won't have to match up your correspondence.

If an agent requests a full manuscript, find out approximately how long the reading will take and call or write if you haven't heard within a week or two of that time. A six- to eight-week turnaround is typical, but agents vary in how quickly they process submissions. If you haven't heard in eight to ten weeks and are not satisfied with the reason why—a vacation or business trip slows an agent down—ask for the manuscript back.

Don't call because you think nudging will speed up the process. Agents receive a constant stream of queries, proposals, and manuscripts. Priority is given to those from clients and then, unless a submission catches his or her fancy, an agent plows through the rest in chronological order.

Bad News Bared

If an agent rejects your query or manuscript, go on to the next agent. Assume the agent was wrong but don't expect an explanation about why your submission was rejected.

"I know it's not perfect," you may be tempted to reply, "but how am I going to make it better if agents won't tell me what's wrong with it?"

To which an agent (or editor) who doesn't charge a fee would respond: "Telling you what's wrong with it is not my job until we're working together. You've already wasted my time by making me read something I can't use. Whether it's trashy or it's classy and just not my cup of tea doesn't make any difference. Maybe I just woke up on the wrong side of the bed this morning. But why should I waste more time telling you why and risk giving you the impression I want to start a dialogue? All I really want is to find the next salable manuscript as quickly as possible. After making million-dollar deals and having my judgment vindicated by rave reviews and runaway sales, discovering good new writers is the most exciting and satisfying part of my job. That's how I make my living. I don't have to be right about your manuscript, and I hope for your sake I'm wrong. But you're not paying me, so I do have the right to minimize the time I waste and the right to be wrong in peace."

Getting Together

It's been said that 70 percent of what is remembered when you talk to someone is not what you say but everything else about you—your appearance, the tone of your voice, and your friendliness. So if an agent likes your work and wants to represent you, meet the agent if you can. It will be easier for you to size up an agent and establish a rapport in person than over the phone. Visiting will also give you the chance to see the office and the books the agent has sold, and meet the staff.

There's no certainty that your courtship will lead to a happy working marriage, but prospects for a successful relationship will be enhanced if at the outset you are familiar with your agent's experience, personality, and operating procedures. You should know what the agent will do for you and what you need from the agent.

Friendliness, for example, is a quality essential for some people but unimportant for others. A writer once gushed to me about her (well-known) agent: "I love him. He's the only person I know who's meaner than I am." One of the top agents in the business once told me that he had no interest in being friends with his clients. His job was to make money for them, and that was his sole concern. If you want a killer shark in your corner, find one.

A new writer is particularly susceptible to being taken advantage of by a bad agent, a fate worse than having no agent at all. Research the agency you are approaching. *Literary Agents of North America* answers some of the following questions, so it may not be necessary to ask all of them. But once an agent agrees to take you on, before you agree to be represented, satisfy yourself, as you would before accepting any kind of professional help, that the agent can and wants to represent you.

The bigger agents are and the more modest the books they are asked to represent, the less agreeable they will be about having to prove themselves to a new writer. In any case, no agent welcomes the third degree. But if the agency is relatively new, questions such as these will help you find out about the agent's personality and credentials:

How long have you been in business?
How did you become an agent?
Do you enjoy being an agent? Why?
Are you a member of SAR or ILAA?
How many books have you sold?
What sales have you made lately?
To what publishers?
What kinds of books do you handle?
Have you sold any like mine?
How many editors and publishers do you deal with?
How large is your staff?
How many clients do you handle?
How do you handle film and foreign rights?
What are your most successful books?
What subsidiary-rights sales have you made?
Since personal relationships with editors are essential, if the agent
    is outside of New York, ask: How often do you go to New York?

Taken together, the answers to these questions should help you determine whether you are talking to an experienced agent.

These questions will help define your working relationship:

What is your commission?
Do you have an agency agreement?
Do you maintain a separate account for your clients' income?
How do you handle expenses?
What records will you maintain on my work?
Do you receive a commission on short pieces I sell?
What are the chances of your selling my book?
How long do you think it will take?
How many potential publishers are there for the project?
In what format do you think my book should be published?
How much of an advance should I expect for it?
How will you go about placing it?
Does the book have subsidiary rights worth pursuing?
Do you forward rejection slips?

What are your office hours?
When should I expect to hear from you?
Should I communicate with you or someone else in the agency?
Will you read my manuscript before I send it to the editor?
How involved do you get with promotion?
Will I be able to see the records you keep of the income from and expenses for my book?

You don't have to ask these particular questions or limit yourself to them. If an agent promises you the moon, head for the nearest egress. If the agent decides not to represent you and the reason isn't clear, ask why. You may not change the agent's mind, but the feedback may help with your next interview.

Auditions

Should you interview more than one agent before making a choice? Interviews will help you decide, but they will also waste all but one agent's time. If you are approaching new agents whose ability you are unsure of, it would be justified. But the folks at Curtis Brown, for instance have already proven themselves, and don't need to audition. Check on an agent before you submit your writing, and when one wants to work with you, reassure yourself about that agent's personality. That said, if an agent accepts your approaching others at the same time, go to it.

Talking to an agent's clients may also not be helpful. For one thing, agents may not want their writers bothered by prospective clients looking for recommendations. Present clients are going to be happy with their agents, which is why they're still clients. Writers who have left their agents may be unfairly biased against them and unable to provide you with an objective assessment. And you may encounter writers who have had wonderful or horrendous experiences with the same agent.

How Not to Get an Agent

If your book is not well enough conceived and written, you won't get an agent for it, no matter how hard you try. But your manuscript is salable, so all you have to do is avoid these tried-and-true mistakes writers make in approaching agents. They range in severity from pet peeves to grounds for homicide. Don't:

Start a query letter with "Dear Sir/Madam" or "To whom it may concern"
Send a handwritten query letter
Offer a laundry list of projects, instead of just pitching the best one or two and mentioning that you have more work available

Send manuscript or illustrations on odd-size or colored paper
Send material bound
Submit a whole manuscript without asking permission
Send material the agent doesn't handle
Send a manuscript filled with typos, preceded by a covering letter
    with a plea to "please excuse the lousy typing"
Send a manuscript with errors in spelling, punctuation, or grammar
Turn a page upside down in the middle of a manuscript to make sure
    that the agent has read it
Forget to include an address or phone number
Copyright a manuscript because of your concern about its being
    stolen. Your work is automatically copyrighted from the moment
    it exists. Author paranoia makes a writer look like an amateur.
Contact an agent because you're "thinking about writing a novel."
    Call or write when you have something to sell.
Call to see if a manuscript arrived, instead of enclosing a postcard or
    arranging for a return receipt
Call an agent at home, at night, or on weekends or holidays without
    first getting permission
Call an agent while you're under the influence
Be dishonest about your work or yourself
Submit work without indicating which agents and publishers have
    seen it
Submit work that has been rejected by everyone except your mother
Send an envelope marked "Personal," when it's business
Seal the back of an envelope with a label that reads:

A Writer's Plea

> This query that you will shortly see
> was written just for you, by little ol' me.
> There's one small favor that I HUMBLY ASK
> Read it before you toss it in the trash!!!

(Fortunately, this young woman's prose was more salable than her
    poetry, and we were able to place her book.)

Take rejection personally and be rude
Threaten. My partner, Elizabeth, once got a call from a woman who
    insisted that she had sent her manuscript six weeks before and
    hadn't received a response. She warned Elizabeth that her son
    was a lawyer, and threatened to "take steps" if the book was lost.
    It turned out that the manuscript was a novella mailed only three
    weeks earlier. We don't handle novellas, but even if we did, she
    would have had to find another agent.

Expect special treatment because your manuscript is "better" than anyone's else's; avoid hype

Forget to enclose an SASE

Send a small reply envelope instead of a #10, which is large enough for an 8½-by-11-inch letter

Try to prove that an agent's negative reaction is wrong

Call to inform an agent that the submission you discussed on the phone has been delayed. Agents don't sit around wondering about the status of submissions they haven't received from writers they don't represent

Pester an agent with phone calls or letters

Trust answering machines. If you don't get an answer to a message left on an answering machine, assume it's the machine's fault, and try a second time. On the other hand, we've gotten calls from writers who told us everything we wanted to know except their phone numbers!

Have unrealistic expectations about your book

Expect to use your advance to pay next month's rent

Ask to meet with an agent or discuss your work before your material has been read

Turn up unexpectedly on an agent's doorstep. Always make an appointment

Be unwilling to follow an agent's reasonable judgment about how your manuscript should be revised or sold

Rules for the Road

Be as professional in approaching an agent as you are in your writing and as you expect an agent to be with you. Whatever an agent says or does should make as much sense to you as it does to the agent. As with your writing or when you hire any professional, you must trust your instincts and your common sense.

Don't be defensive in dealing with your agent. Although you should never abuse your agent's time, always remember who works for whom. But at the same time, remember that, until your agent sells something for you, he or she is working for free. So keep tabs on what's happening with your manuscript, but tread lightly.

CHAPTER FIVE

The Agency Contract: Prenuptial Agreements

A verbal agreement ain't worth the paper it's printed on.
—Samuel Goldwyn

In the past, agents preferred handshake agreements. Many still do. But written agreements are becoming more common. Large agencies have always had them, and movie agents in California are required by law to have them.

Agents who prefer not to have a contract believe that trust is the foundation of the author-agent relationship. If agent and author trust each other, no contract is necessary. If they don't, it's time to get a divorce. New agents often start out feeling this way, and then decide to have a written agreement to protect themselves, after an author has left them without justification. The law offers more protection to the writer than the agent, so not having a written agreement places a greater risk on the agent.

Agents who rely on oral agreements know that when they sell a book, their rights are protected by the agent's clause. Chapter 10 discusses this clause, and a sample appears in Appendix A.

However, any arrangement, written or oral, is only as binding as the good faith of the people who agree to it. If an agent, author, or publisher wants to be dishonest, figuring out how is easy.

Biting the House that Feeds You

An editor once told us that his company had signed an agreement with a writer and paid the first part of the advance. The author got sick and spent the advance but failed to deliver the manuscript. He asked the publisher to give him the second half of the advance so he could finish the book. The publisher was sympathetic to the writer's plight and sent him the rest of the advance. When the writer still didn't complete the book, the publisher sued to recoup the advance. The writer won the case, claiming that the publisher had waived the right to recover the advance by paying the second half of the advance before it was due!

The Dotted Line

Some agents supplement their oral understandings with a letter of agreement. You or your agent can give an oral agreement the force of a contract by typing up the points you agree on and then making sure that both of you have dated copies of it bearing both of your signatures.

Whether you accept a written or oral agreement with your agent will depend on how your agent operates and your preference. Even if your agent doesn't use a contract, he or she should be willing to draw one up and sign it if it's important to you.

It's impossible for an agency or a publishing agreement to provide for every contingency that can befall a relationship or a book, but it can cover the basics and thus help to avoid misunderstandings that lead to problems. Your agreement should spell out the obligations of both you and your agent while the agreement lasts and after it ends. It should also include the means for ending the relationship.

Questions about the agent-author relationship don't arise when all is well. But when a real or imagined problem crops up, writers wonder what their obligations are to their agents. One of life's lessons is that you avoid problems by minimizing risks. When your future or large amounts of money may be at stake, do you want to rely solely on your assumptions, your memory, and the goodwill of your agent to protect your interests? A working marriage consummated with a mutually satisfactory agreement helps avoid problems and provides the means to solve those that do arise.

Nineteen Steps to a Clear Understanding

Just as no two agents are alike, no two agency agreements are the same. They vary in length, thoroughness, clarity (some are written in legalese, others as a letter between author and agent), tone, and, of course, the terms they cover.

Your ability to change an agreement will depend on your value as a writer and how much an agent wants to represent you. But even if you are a new writer approaching your first agent, you are entitled to an agreement that you think is fair, and you should settle for nothing less. The contract that is right for you is the one that you and your agent decide is right for both of you.

Whatever form your agreement takes, you and your agent should reach an understanding on the following nineteen points:

1. *The confirmation of your agent.* Unless you and your agent agree otherwise, your agent will expect to have the exclusive right to sell all of your work and your literary services throughout the world. This means that even you can't sell your own work; only your agent can. If a publisher asks you to write a book or offers you a contract, you are obligated not to discuss terms, and to refer the publisher to your agent.

This clause may mention the agent's right to make his or her services available to others in any capacity and to hire coagents who are specialists to help with subsidiary rights such as film or foreign rights.

The compact between you and your agent creates a fiduciary responsibility on your agent's part. Your agent is obligated to act with a high degree of responsibility in representing you and your work.

Agents have two big incentives: They want to keep clients and they want to make money, which they do by placing their writers' work. Nonetheless, whether your agreement says so or not, you have the right to expect honesty, confidentiality, and a professional effort on your agent's part.

2. *What your agent will represent.* An agreement can be limited to specific projects or kinds of writing or to a specific territory, such as North America. But an agent will normally expect to have the right of first refusal on all of a client's work in all forms: books, plays, screenplays, essays, articles, short stories, poetry, and software in all print, broadcast, electronic, and merchandising media throughout the world. This includes material you write or coauthor.

The exceptions to this include work that is already committed to another agent or buyer, writing you produce as part of your job, and other projects or kinds of writing you and the agent agree to exclude.

For example, if you are a screenwriter and you already have an agent for your screenplays, the agent you find to sell your novel may agree to exclude screenwriting (and perhaps motion-picture rights to your novels) from the agreement. Or if your agent wants to represent your novels, but you also write poetry, articles, or short stories, which the agent doesn't handle, you should be free to sell them on your own or through another agent.

Since the agent is trying to establish your reputation and may not be making any money in the attempt, or since the agent's efforts have made your other work more salable, the agent may want commissions on work that you sell for yourself or through another agent. You will have to settle this issue in a spirit of fairness to both of you.

3. *How long the agreement will last.* Oral agreements tend to continue only as long as both parties want them to. This may be true of written agreements also. They may last indefinitely, with the writer given the right to end the agreement with thirty or sixty days' notice. This is, in effect, a one-book contract, because it leaves you free to go elsewhere with your next book.

The usual alternative is for an agreement to last for a period of time—one, two, three, or even five years—after which the writer can cancel the agreement or let it be extended automatically for the same period of time.

The premise of a long-term contract is that it may take years to establish a writer, and the agreement should protect the agent's investment of time, energy, and out-of-pocket expenses.

4. *Competitive books.* An agency agreement may include a clause allowing the agent to handle books competitive with yours. Agents vary in their willingness to represent competitive books.

Timing may be the determining factor. If an agent is trying to sell two competitive books at the same time, the agent is faced with the problem of which editors to show which project to and in what order. The same problem may arise in selling first-serial and subsidiary rights. Also, part of an agent's fiduciary responsibility is to inform clients about potential conflicts of interest.

If one of the books has already been sold or published, handling a second book on the subject may not impair the agent's effectiveness in representing the first book. But if a second project is clearly competitive with one an agent is already handling, the agent must notify the writers and publishers involved. If both clients are agreeable, the agent should be free to sell the second manuscript. Whether two projects will be competitive and what to do about it is a judgment call, and an honest agent will make the right decision.

Certainly, the second author will benefit from the agent's experience with similar books. Publishers who were outbid for the first book may be interested in the second. On the other hand, if an agent has tried unsuccessfully to sell a book like the one you're proposing, the agent may be able to save you time at the outset by telling you to go on to the next project.

5. *The commission.* This will specify your agent's commission, usually 10 or 15 percent, although some agents charge 12½ percent, and some, if they provide editorial assistance, as much as 25 percent.

If your agent uses a network of foreign agents to handle foreign sales, it will specify the foreign agents' commission on such sales, usually 10 percent, which will bring the total commission on foreign sales to 20-25 percent.

Agents usually split their normal commission with their movie agents, but may add 5-10 percent for their coagents, bringing the total commission to no higher than 20 percent.

The commission clause may also indicate that commissions earned by the agent do not have to be returned for any reason. For example, if an agent sells a book, receives the commission on the first part of the advance, and either the author doesn't deliver the manuscript or the publisher decides it's not satisfactory and the author must return the advance, what should the agent do?

Nothing. The agent has done his or her job by selling the manuscript. If the writer doesn't produce or the manuscript is unsatisfactory, it's not the agent's fault, so why should the agent be penalized by having to return the commission? This is a black-and-white situation.

Other circumstances may not be so simple, however, and, regardless of this provision, an agent may be willing to return a commission if the author repays an advance and the circumstances warrant it. Some agents take the position that if the writer has acted responsibly, the agent will repay the commission when the writer returns the advance.

6. The agent as funnel. Another reason many agents are comfortable with oral agreements is that they know that when they sell a book, the contract will include a clause naming them as the agent for the book. As explained earlier, this clause enables your agent to receive the money you earn, deduct a commission, and forward the balance to you. Publishers prefer this system because agents protect them from writers claiming they never received money due them and because agents serve as knowledgeable mediators if questions arise. And of course, as conduits for an author's income, agents are certain to receive commissions.

When agents have generated enough income, they usually maintain a separate account, so that their clients' income won't be mingled with their own. The money in this account belongs to the agent's clients, not the agency, so that if the agency goes bankrupt, client income is safe. This is a standard practice not usually mentioned in an agency agreement, but you should feel free to confirm it. New agents may not have a separate account because they may not receive enough checks to warrant opening one. State laws about bank accounts also vary.

7. Remittance time. Dorothy Parker once said that the two most beautiful words in the English language are "Check enclosed." This clause specifies how soon your agent will forward your income and royalty statements to you after receiving them. Ten working days is generally enough time for checks to clear in an agent's bank. However, a check in a foreign currency may take months to clear.

8. Expenses. An agent will pay for local phone calls and ordinary mailing expenses. Your agent may expect you to pay for part or all of the other expenses, such as long-distance phone calls, cables, telex messages, overseas mailings, photocopying proposals or manuscripts, buying bound galleys and books, messengers, and legal advice.

As mentioned earlier, agents who charge a 15 percent commission may absorb some expenses usually charged to writers. An agency agreement indicates who pays for which expenses and when.

Whether or not it's stated, it's understood that your agent will not commit you to a large expense without your approval.

9. Checking the books. You are legally entitled to examine the entries in your agent's books relating to the income from and expenses for your work. If your agent is absorbing expenses, there will be no need to check them, and there may be no books to check. You should receive an itemized list of the expenses deducted from your income. If an agent resists your right to see the financial records being maintained on your behalf, head for the nearest exit.

If you are receiving royalty statements with your checks, then you know the source of the income and how the amount on the check was calculated. At tax time, you will receive a tax form listing your total earnings for the previous year.

Just as your agent will, you must always check all of the numbers on your statements carefully, and you must not hesitate to ask about anything that isn't clear to you. You and your agent have an identical interest in making sure that you get every cent you've earned. But ultimately, the responsibility for your money is yours.

10. Your freedom to sign the agreement. This clause indicates that you are free to sell your work and sign the agency agreement. It protects the agent from conflicts caused by a previous buyer or agent.

11. Your agent's freedom to assign the agreement. If you sign up with a large agency and your agent leaves, you will be assigned to another agent. If you are unhappy with the new agent, you are free to request an agent you are comfortable with or leave the agency.

Your agent does not have the right to transfer you as a client to another agency without your approval if he or she sells out, moves on to something new, or passes away. However, like you, your agent has the right to assign income to others.

12. Your freedom to pass the agreement on. Although the relationship between a writer and agent ends if either of you dies or is incapacitated, the agreement may state, as a publishing agreement does, that its terms are binding on your heirs or anyone to whom you give the proceeds of the book. Continuing income from authors' estates can be a major source of regular income for an agent. And knowing that one's literary affairs will be well taken care of after one has crossed the bar can be a source of comfort for writers.

13. Which state law governs the agreement. This clause says that the agreement will be interpreted according to the laws of the state in which your agency has its headquarters.

14. Changing the agreement. As your career develops, what you need from an agent may change. For example, you write nonfiction books and your agreement states that your agent will handle all of your work, but you now want to write children's books, an area in which your agent has no interest or experience. You should be free to sell your children's books yourself or find another agent for them, if your agent can't find one for you.

Your agent may also want to alter the agreement. At first, for instance, your agent may not want to handle your short stories or articles. Why? There are three reasons:

- A 10 or 15 percent commission may not compensate your agent sufficiently for the time spent placing a short piece.
- Newspapers and magazines have a price range for free-lance material. An agent can't up the ante enough to justify handling it. Once you start dealing with editors and talking to writers about their experiences, you will get a sense of how your work fits into a periodical's price range.
- Since you are basically trying to sell only first-time North American rights to the piece for a one-time payment, the negotiations are much simpler than they would be for a book. Consequently, you have less need of an agent's services, especially if you are a journalist who has already set up your own contacts with editors. However, if your articles or short stories consistently command four-figure sums, your agent may be willing to become involved with your short pieces.

This clause states that you and your agent must sign all changes and additions to the agreement between you, and that each of you has a signed, dated copy of the agreement. The foregoing examples are situations simple enough to be settled by a meeting or a phone call.

15. When your marriage is threatened. In case a marital spat does come between you and your agent, the agreement should provide a method for resolving it. The simplest way is for you and your agent to agree to discuss the problem, in person, by phone, or by mail. If you both conscientiously try to solve the problem in a way that is fair to each of you, you will find an equitable solution to most problems.

For a problem the two of you can't handle, consider one of these alternatives:

- Agreeing to accept the judgment of a mediator on whom you and your agent agree. This person can be a judicious, knowledgeable publishing professional or an experienced mediator, whom you can find through the publishing, arts, or legal community.
- Using an arbitrator from an organization that supplies them. The best known of these groups is the American Arbitration Association. This approach can be less time-consuming, costly, and technical than using a lawyer, but, as with a mediator, the results

hinge on how competent and knowledgeable the person is.
- The longest, most painful, and potentially the most expensive possibility is hiring a lawyer. Since anyone can hire a lawyer at any time, this possibility doesn't have to be mentioned in the agreement.

16. *Getting a friendly divorce.* The beginning of your working marriage with your agent can be a honeymoon, when everything is fine because you're both on your best behavior. The agent is submitting your book and you are both eager with anticipation. If the book sells, you're both delighted, because it proves the two of you were right about the book and each other.

If it doesn't, the agent's interest may wane. You may realize that although you were right about your book, you were wrong about your agent. This could happen after a month or a year. It could happen with the first book or the twelfth.

It could happen if your book becomes a best seller and you decide that you need a larger agency, a lawyer to negotiate contracts, or both. One of the unhappy realities of publishing is the R&D factor: successful writers switching from the small agencies and publishers that develop their marketability to big agencies and publishers.

If the time to leave your agent does come, you won't want to prolong the relationship or slow down the progress of your career. You must make the transition to another agent as quickly and painlessly as possible, so you can get on with selling your work.

Even with a big agency or an established agent, the problem is not whether the agent is capable but how soon you can leave the agency should you decide to do so.

You can end your agency relationship at any time. An agreement with no fixed duration will provide for ending the relationship with a certified letter in a certain period of time, usually thirty or sixty days. This allows time for submissions to be sold or returned and for the agent to notify coagents to wind up their activities. It will also give you time to mull over your decision and look for another agent.

But if you are between books, and your agent isn't involved in selling your work, a thirty- or sixty-day waiting period may not be necessary. Ask for an immediate release.

If the agreement runs for a specific time period, you can terminate it at the end of that period. Otherwise, the agreement will be automatically extended for the same amount of time. If you end a fixed-term agreement without cause before it expires, you may be liable for commissions the agent would have earned had the agreement run its course.

17. *After you separate.* This clause defines your agent's rights and responsibilities after the agreement ends. Usually the agent will continue to receive an author's income from sales already concluded. However, if you prefer, your agent will probably not object if you arrange with your publisher to have separate checks and statements sent to you and your agent.

In any event, your agent has the right to receive the commission on all projects already sold and those on which negotiations began while the agent represented you. Because negotiations, especially those involving movies, big books, or big publishers may drag on, the agreement may allow the agent to receive a commission on a sale if the negotiations for it began while the agent represented you and end within a fixed period, maybe six months, after the agreement terminates.

Just as it is part of your agent's fiduciary responsibility to inform you about all offers, your agent must also, upon request, return manuscripts you have submitted and furnish you with copies of rejection letters. The letters will be helpful if you decide to pursue the sale of your book, since you or your next agent will not want to submit your manuscript to an editor who has already rejected it.

18. Subsidiary rights. Another issue to resolve when you leave your agent is the sale of subsidiary rights. If an agent has placed a novel for you, will he or she be allowed to continue to represent the book for film and foreign rights that may not materialize for decades?

If the agent had let the publisher keep all of the book's subsidiary rights, then the agent would share in them, because he or she continues to receive commissions on all sales for which you have signed contracts. However, your agent usually tries to retain subsidiary rights for you so your publisher won't take a bite out of the proceeds and so the agent can sell those rights. Agents need sub rights income to help sustain their agencies. Since your agent made those rights sales possible by the initial sale of your book, and then kept those rights out of the publisher's hands for you, he or she may feel entitled to keep representing such rights, or at least to receive commissions on them regardless of who makes the sales.

The film or foreign rights to a book may be more valuable than the American book sales. Agents make a living by encouraging writers who produce not just one book but many books, with bookstore-sales as well as subsidiary-rights potential. This potential may grow over time, as the author's career develops and new rights, like software, come into being.

If, for example, you become a famous novelist, the foreign and film rights for your previous books may become valuable. If you've written a nonfiction book that's gone out of print, and your agent has had the rights for the book reverted to you, renewed interest in the subject may make it possible to get the book republished.

If you are leaving your agent because he or she didn't pursue subsidiary-rights sales with sufficient vigor, the former agent may be willing to split commissions with the new one. The trade-off here is that although your first agent will make less money, the income will come in with no effort or expense on that agent's part. The alternatives are to see if your new agent will accept half of the normal commission, or to pay two full commissions, which will be worth it if you're getting 5 or 10 percent less of something rather than a larger percentage of nothing.

On the other hand, even though you've left, your first agent will still want to sell the subsidiary rights for previously sold books as quickly and for as much money as possible. It's also conceivable that your new agent is working with at least some of the same movie and foreign coagents as your first agent, so there may be no advantage in trying to withdraw subsidiary rights from the first one.

19. Sales after the divorce. To stop authors from jumping ship to avoid paying a commission, some agents have a clause stating that they will receive commissions on all sales that take place within a certain time, perhaps three months, after the agreement ends.

The dissolution of your working marriage is an important part of your agreement with your agent, and you ought to be certain that it is worked out to your mutual satisfaction.

Two Clauses to Avoid in an Agency Agreement
Because no recognized standards exist for agency agreements, there is no definitive agency contract by which you can judge the one an agent presents to you. You have to be a careful consumer, just as you would when signing any business document.

Your agent should be willing to explain any clauses that are not clear to you and to change anything that both of you agree should be altered to suit your circumstances. If you have concerns about an agreement and the agent isn't willing to discuss them or make what you feel are reasonable changes, talk to other professionals in your publishing network or consider hiring an attorney who knows publishing, to go over the agreement with you.

What is right in your agreement with your agent is whatever you and your agent agree to in a spirit of trust and good faith. Nevertheless, be wary of the following two provisions in an agency agreement:

1. A monthly retainer fee. Writers risk their time writing their books, and agents risk theirs by trying to sell them. If the book doesn't sell, both are out the time, effort, and expenses they lost on the project. This has always been the premise of the writing and agenting professions.

However, some agents charge monthly retainer fees to help minimize their risk. If you can afford to subsidize your agent and are otherwise satisified with the agent's honesty, reputation, experience, and ability, then it's up to you to decide whether you should pay your agent a salary.

2. *Fees for expenses.* Some agents ask authors to help pay for expenses such as visits to editors, and dinners with them. This is another unjustified form of subsidy unless you can afford it and it comes out of the agent's first commission.

A Modest Proposal

The information in this chapter can't be the final word, but it will provide a basis for understanding your relationship with your agent, for discussing questions if they arise, and for going your separate ways as painlessly as possible.

Regardless of what this book recommends, you should work with an agent whom you like and respect, and in whose ability you have confidence. Your working arrangement with your agent should be whatever you and your agent agree is fair.

The agency agreements in Appendix B will give you an idea of what such agreements look like. If you trust your instincts, use your common sense, and act in good faith, you will be doing your part in establishing a lasting, satisfying working marriage with your agent.

CHAPTER SIX

When the Honeymoon Is Over

First Actor: "What should I get my agent for Christmas?"
Second Actor: "A cattle prod."

—Your Film Acting Career

Congratulations! Your agent has sold your book. Your future looks bright and your working marriage with your agent has been blessed with a deal that binds you both to your publisher and to each other.

As with any marriage, the challenge now is to make your working marriage with your agent as fruitful and rewarding as possible. How can you keep your agent happy? Try these eleven steps to a happy marriage:

1. Write well. Write your books as well as possible. Since, like editors, agents reject more than 90 percent of the material they receive, just getting a proposal or manuscript in the mail that they know will be well conceived, well written, and professionally submitted is a source of relief and pleasure.

Also remember that an agent's credibility is on the line with every submission.

2. Deliver your book on time. There are enough hassles getting a book published well. Unless you have no alternative, don't add to them and risk a rejection by being late with your manuscript.

3. Develop your AR. Your AR is your agent reflex. It means that if an editor approaches you and wants to buy your book or wants you to write one, talk about the book but not about the money. Memorize this line, and use it : "Gee, that sounds great, but if you want to talk about money, you'd better call my agent." Here's hoping you need it often!

Even after your book is sold, don't talk to your editor about money without asking your agent. You may do yourself more harm than good.

4. Fight back with your AR. The moment you have a problem with your book, your editor, or your publisher that you can't handle, use your AR.

Your agent is involved with other books and clients. Don't assume he or she knows about the problem. Don't delay, hoping it might go away by itself. Don't beat your head against a wall trying to find the solution by yourself. Don't hesitate to call or write, as our writers have sometimes done because they didn't want to bother us. Part of an agent's value is his or her experience. Maybe your agent has already dealt with the problem before and knows how to solve it. He or she may be able to show you why it really isn't a problem, or why it's an opportunity in disguise.

Calling your agent about every small frustration will damage your relationship. But if you have a serious concern, tell your agent about it immediately.

5. *Live and help live.* One of the joys of the agenting business is that agents can work in any way that they wish and that their writers will accept. When you start working with your agent, agree on how your agent will go about sending out your work and whether one or more copies will be submitted at a time. Once you establish a mutually satisfactory way of working with your agent, be patient. If it becomes ineffective, change it.

6. *Communicate only when necessary.* Another point to settle when your agent starts to submit your work is when you can expect to hear from him or her. Unless it's for social or personal reasons such as suggesting an evening out or needing advice on a family matter, call or write your agent only when it's necessary. Between the mail and the phone, agents are subjected to hundreds of communications a week. Contact your agent only if you have a legitimate reason to do so. When you do contact your agent, be cheerful and optimistic; ask if there's any way you can help.

7. *Forget about your manuscript.* Once your agent begins submitting your manuscript, try to forget it exists. Unless you have a timely or outstanding project, expect Murphy's Law of Time to set in: Things always take longer than you want them to. Publishing is a slow business. Even after your book is sold, you may have to wait a month or more for a contract, and just as long for the first part of your advance.

You and your agent both want to sell your book as quickly as possible, and your agent will be delighted to call you with good news the moment there is any to report. Meanwhile, do one of three things:
- If you have a brainstorm on how to improve your manuscript and your agent agrees with you, revise it and get it back to the agent quickly.
- If your book isn't finished and you have faith that it will sell, continue to work on it.
- Start your next book.

8. Celebrate when your book is sold. If your agent sells your book, show your appreciation. A bottle of champagne or a celebratory meal at a favorite restaurant will do nicely. You don't have to spend a fortune, and your agent will appreciate your thoughtfulness. Elizabeth once received a beautiful bouquet of flowers because a writer was delighted with Elizabeth's rejection letter!

9. Acknowledge your agent. Like most people, agents like to see their names in print. Thanking your agent in your dedication or acknowledgments will bring added pride and pleasure to your agent every time he or she thinks about your book. When people ask Elizabeth and me if we have children, we say no, we have books instead. Your book is certainly your baby, but, like you, it's also part of your agent's extended literary family.

10. Promote your books. Two cannibals are having dinner and one says to the other: "You know, I don't like your publisher."

"OK," the other cannibal replies, "then just eat the noodles."

The most common reason authors are unhappy with their publishers is lack of promotion. Unless a book is one of the few big titles on a list, an author will usually be dissatisfied with what the publisher is doing to promote the book.

A promotable author is the (pun intended) best selling tool a publisher has. But many authors can't promote their books; others won't— and without a news angle or a famous or promotable personality behind it, a novel is tougher to publicize than nonfiction.

If you are published by a large house, and your book is not getting top-of-the-line treatment, it will be one of many. Assume that no one knows or cares as much about your book as you do, and that only your editor has read it. Assume that communications between the advertising, editorial, publicity, and sales departments are not perfect. All this means that if you want the public to find out about your book, you either have to let fate take its course or work damn hard to promote it.

Publishers plan promotion months in advance of publication to have maximum impact at the time of publication, when books arrive in the stores and reviews appear.

By the time your book is published, your publisher is busy planning for the future. The momentum that builds for a book has either developed or dissipated, and it's too late to do much at that point except wait and see how reviewers and buyers respond to the book.

Getting Your Promotion in Motion

Every book is a book yet each one is an individual combination of author, content, publisher, timing, price, design, format, editor, and competition inside and outside of the house. The three basic resources you have are your publisher, your book, and you.

The following suggestions will provide a logical approach to promoting your book:

• From the moment you decide to write your book, use your imagination to think about ways your book can be promoted. Promotion involves a way of thinking about how to make your book successful. Cultivate the knack of thinking in an original, promotional, anything-is-possible way. Develop a reflex for thinking of how you can use every person or event that comes along to promote you or your book.

• Write your ideas down and stick them in a promotion file. Your agent can be a creative sounding board for ideas.

• Mine the promotion chapters in books about publishing and self-publishing. Stories in *Writer's Digest*, *The Writer*, and *PW* will also yield ideas.

• Have a promotion potluck like we do at the beginning of the year for writers with books coming out that year. Invite writers and members of the book community and have a brainstorming session on one another's books. You will come up with contacts and ideas.

• Expand your professional network. Chat with writers, booksellers, marketing experts, sales reps, and reviewers about promotion techniques they find effective and how these ideas can be applied to your book.

Word of mouth remains the best advertising. Your personal and professional networks can be an effective national force generating "The Big Mo": momentum. One of the reasons that Jacqueline Susann was a life-time member of the best-seller club was that her Christmas mailing list contained 9,000 names. She worked hard at making friends in the business, and it paid off in sales.

• Analyze the nature, size, and location of the markets for your book and how to reach them as effectively and inexpensively as possible.

• Create a marketing plan for your book, integrating ideas for advertising, sales promotion (in-store selling aids), and publicity. Try it out on your agent, writers, and publishing people. After you've incorporated their suggestions, include the marketing plan when your agent submits your manuscript.

Your editor can share it with the advertising, publicity, and sales people and may use it when presenting your book to the reps at the sales conference. The reps will find the information helpful when selling your book. Your eagerness and ability to get behind your book without making it an ego trip will affect a publisher's decision to buy your book and how strongly they'll back it.

Once your publisher's staff has evaluated the plan, get their reaction to it. Then determine what the publisher will do and decide what you will do about the ideas the publisher doesn't want to pursue.

• Your publisher will send you a publicity form with questions about yourself, your media experience and contacts, and sources for serialization, quotes, and reviews. Fill it out thoroughly.

• Visit your publisher before promotion plans are made. Sell yourself to the staff while asking all the people you can how they think your book can be promoted and how you can help.

• Authors are rarely invited to sales conferences. But if you can dazzle the sales reps with your book or yourself, suggest the idea to your editor.

• Attend the American Booksellers Association convention. The hoopla and the sheer number of books at the ABA will be an enlightening if humbling experience. You will also find techniques for promoting your book. You'll probably have to pay your way to the convention, but your editor or publicist may be willing to arrange for an author's badge to get you onto the floor.

• If your publisher wants to wait and see what happens after the book is published, create a test-market promotion campaign where you live or in the nearest medium-sized city. If your efforts produce sales, your publisher should be willing to push your book.

• If your publisher is reluctant to do publicity, consider hiring your own publicist. Your agent may be able to suggest an experienced pro. Your publisher may be willing to share the cost or advance you the money and charge all or part of it against your royalties, or pick up the tab if the book sells a certain number of copies. Other alternatives include bartering with your publicist for all or part of the cost, or doing part of the work to lessen the fee, or just using a publicist as a consultant and doing the work yourself.

How to Promote Your Book

Luck aside, five elements are needed for effective publicity: an interesting idea, a good book, a promotable personality, professional-looking publicity materials, and the efficient planning and execution of a campaign.

Let's assume you have the first three, and discuss the fourth and fifth. The tools you need for publicity are a telephone, books, a press kit, and media lists.

A press kit can include anything that you think will impress the media, but it usually contains a news release, a list of interview topics you can discuss even if they have nothing to do with the book, a one-page bio, a photo of you, reviews from major media, and a pitch letter tying this material together and explaining why you will make a good interview.

Press kits are sent with books to radio and television talk show producers and to book-review and feature editors at newspapers, magazines, and wire services to obtain interviews.

If you want to begin your publicity campaign in a simple way, send just a news release, a list of interview topics, and a book. Your publisher will have media lists, and libraries usually have media directories. Cable TV, special-interest trade and consumer media, and computer networking are part of the reason why there are more opportunities to promote your book than ever before.

Call your publisher whenever there's good news and follow up with a letter to your editor and your publicist as well as sending reviews and new ideas. Be relentless, but always be professional.

Access to publicity is an equalizer among publishers. The media need colorful personalities, good copy, and busy call-in lines. They don't care who supplies them. In promoting their books, writers and publishers are not so much limited by their budgets as they are by their imagination, energy, and persistence.

For a thorough and comprehensive guide to publicizing your book, read Peggy Glenn's *Publicity for Books and Authors*.

The Big Day

• When your book is published, have a party. If a book-signing has been arranged, don't dilute the interest and publicity it will generate with a party of your own. But if it won't conflict with other plans, celebrate!

If you can, pick a spot for your party that relates to your book. Invite your personal and professional networks, publicity media, anyone in the book community who can help, and opinion makers. Not everybody will come, but a good-looking invitation will let your community know about your book. Your publisher may agree to pay for the party or part of it.

• Try to think of an event that you can stage or that you can be part of that will tie in to your book and attract the media's attention.

• Participate in panels, lectures, seminars, conventions, writers' and academic conferences. Contact community organizations, either to talk about your book or about writing it, or about anything else as long as you can plug your book. Sell books if you can.

• If you can get paid to speak, take your act on the road. Set up or hire a lecture agent to arrange for appearances just after publication in as many major book markets as you have the stamina for. Let your publisher know your itinerary as far in advance as possible. The publicity department should be willing to contact the media in those cities to let them know when you'll be available.

• Other ways to publicize your book include T-shirts, printing the title and publisher on your letterhead, business cards, Christmas cards, and bookmarks on which you can list all of your books. Just walking around holding your book will make it a conversation piece.

• Stay alert for unexpected promotional opportunities and seize every chance to get your book in the public eye. Your publisher has books sitting in the warehouse not earning their keep. If you can show them how to put the books to good use, they will usually be willing to oblige.

 • Be synergistic. Recycle the ideas in your books in as many forms as possible: talks, articles, other books, audio and video cassettes, electronic media. The cumulative impact of all of your work will increase your sales and your value as an author.

The Big Picture

Take the long view about promotion. Look at it as a lifelong challenge at which you will become more effective with each book. When reporters and talk-show hosts invite you back, and your promotional efforts boost the sales of your book, you will find the process exciting.

Trying to convince millions of book buyers across the country to buy your book will probably be the hardest thing you have ever done, much harder than writing your book. So set realistic goals for what to expect of your book and yourself.

And don't get involved with promotion half-heartedly. You've got to convince yourself and your publisher that you harbor a consuming lust for success and that you are irresistibly driven to do whatever it takes to make your books sell. Unless you jump into promotion body and soul, you'd be better off working on your next book.

Let your agent help you be realistic about balancing your efforts against the sales they may produce, the enjoyment you get out of promotion, and the need to use your time as productively as possible.

Depending upon your goals, your personality, the kind of books you write, and your need to earn a living, you might be right to decide that you, your publisher, and your readers will be better served if you keep your cheeks glued to a chair and your hands chained to a keyboard.

11. Be faithful to your agent. Agents take on new writers in the hope that they will become better at their craft and more profitable as clients as time goes by. If you have a legitimate reason to switch agents, you should do so without hesitation. But to leave an agent who is doing a good job for you is to rob the agent of future commissions earned partly because of the agent's commitment to your career.

Terminal Transgressions

Your working marriage with your agent will go through a period of adjustment, and you may experience the ups and downs that can befall any continuing relationship. But if you both act in a spirit of trust and good faith and have your share of luck, your marriage will succeed.

On the other hand, even the most promising marriage can turn sour. The day may come when you decide that your agent is wrong for you. If that day comes, it's time to think about divorce.

Other than flagrant violations of professional ethics, what reasons justify leaving your agent? The following points indicate you may have a problem with your agent.

Your agent never contacts you. Don't expect an agent to be constantly checking in with you to make sure everything's okay. However, your agent should inform you promptly about significant developments regarding your work. He or she may only call with good or helpful news, which may be a long time in coming.

At the same time, if you never hear about the progress of your agent's efforts, you may rightly wonder what, if anything, is going on. You can try to avoid this problem by establishing at the outset when you can expect to hear from your agent. If your agent repeatedly fails to abide by the arrangement, find out why and change either the system or the agent.

Your agent is not a mind reader. Call or write if you have a question about your work, but, especially until your agent has sold something for you, don't expect too much in the way of hand-holding.

Your agent fails to respond promptly to letters or phone calls. What would you do if your doctor, lawyer, accountant, or anyone else you hired to work for you didn't return your phone calls? You'd hire someone else.

Agents make their living by mail and by phone. They are extremely sensitive about having their phone calls returned by editors. If your agent likes and respects you and wants to represent you, your letters and calls will be answered. If your agent won't return your calls or respond to your letters, hire one who will.

However, trust your agent—don't get paranoid if you don't receive an instant response. Find out why. Was the agent ill, very busy, out of town? A responsible agent will have a satisfactory explanation. If not, and poor communication becomes a habit, it's time to move on.

Your agent is not actively pursuing the sale of your work. If your manuscript has become a doorstop in your agent's office, it's not doing either of you any good. Find out what the agent plans to do with the project. Has it been seen by all the likely editors? If you have an agent who is not in New York, is he or she waiting to discuss the project with editors in person?

Being locked into a long-term contract makes it easier for an agent to slough off, figuring that, no matter what he or she does or fails to do, the writer's not going anywhere.

Once again, agree at the beginning on the best strategy for selling your book, and if that doesn't work and you or your agent can't come up with a second line of attack, you should be free to pursue the sale of the property yourself or seek another agent.

If we temporarily run out of editors to whom to send a project, we may tell writers to take a shot at selling the book themselves without obligation to us, and if they succeed, they can decide at that time if they want us to negotiate the contract. Meanwhile, if we find a new editor or imprint, or an editor we know changes houses, or we hear about a house needing such a book, we will let the author know we are sending it out.

Keep in mind that sometimes a book only needs time and patience to sell. Whether it's an upswing in handicrafts, a resurgence of interest in category westerns, or a recession, no matter what happens, it's good for somebody and bad for someone else (now, there's a book idea). Even the worst catastrophe can be good for a writer.

Just because your book hasn't sold doesn't inevitably mean that you should switch agents. Writing your next book may be the best course. Time away from it may allow the market for your book to improve, or for you or your agent to come up with a more salable approach to the subject, or for the success of your next book to make unsold work salable.

Agents want to represent authors, not books. They're in it for the long run. They know that even if a first book doesn't sell, a second one will probably be more likely to, making the rest of an author's books, including previously unsold work, more marketable.

Your agent is vague about his or her activities. If your agent doesn't seem to know what's going on with your book or you're not getting definite answers to questions about your work, find out why. If you're not satisfied, find yourself another agent.

Your agent does not want to handle new work. You've written a book or proposal you're very excited about, but your agent either doesn't like it or doesn't think much of its chances. If your agent's arguments about the project's weaknesses don't convince you, what do you do? If it happens once, let your agent continue to handle projects under way and try to sell it yourself. If your agent continues to reject your work, maybe you should be looking for one who's in tune with the direction your work is taking.

Your agent is, despite his or her best efforts, unable to sell your work. Matching your book with the right time for its publication, the right editor, and the right house may take a phone call or, through no fault of either your book or your agent, years. As long as your agent believes in your book and is trying to sell it, he or she deserves the right to keep trying. But if it becomes apparent that your agent no longer cares about your book, then it's time to separate the two of them.

Your agent sells your book and it becomes a blockbuster. Suppose you are a new writer represented by a small new agency and, to everyone's surprise, your first book takes off and hits the best-seller list. If the book's success is just a fluke unlikely to repeat itself, consider yourself lucky.

But if you are a novelist who expects to turn out a string of best sellers, each with strong movie and foreign-rights potential, then you may have outgrown your agent. Best-selling authors sometimes turn to agents like the prodigiously successful Morton Janklow who are also lawyers and perform both functions for their clients. The decision to change agents will be forced upon you, because if you have a best seller, agents will start contacting you.

Two Steps to Freedom

If a problem develops between you and your agent, here are two steps you can take to solve it:

1. Meet with your agent; if that will be too painful, call or write. If your agent has acted conscientiously on your behalf, you owe it to your agent to give him or her a chance to discuss the problem with you.

Make sure that your concern is real and justified. If it is, try to find a mutually satisfactory solution to the problem. If you can't, or if after a fair trial, within a mutually agreeable time period, the solution doesn't work, it's time to end the relationship.

But in fairness to your agent, don't approach or commit yourself to a new agent until you've given your present agent a chance to remedy the situation. Ending a basically sound relationship in a moment of perhaps unjustified pique and turning to a second agent who may turn out to be less satisfactory would not be a wise decision.

2. Notify the agent of your decision, either in person or by sending a certified letter explaining the problem and your decision to end your relationship at the earliest date allowed by the agreement. If you meet with the agent, follow up your conversation with a certified letter confirming any new terms you agree on during your conversation.

If the waiting period required by the contract is longer than sixty days, request that the agreement be terminated at that time anyway. Your agent will probably be willing to release you early rather than hold on to an unwilling, unproductive client, especially if you have a legitimate grievance. If you are dead set on leaving your agent, you can. You may have to consult a literary attorney if your agent offers resistance.

A warning: Publishing is a small world whose denizens thrive on their insatiable appetites for that delectable delicacy: gossip. Avoid becoming known as a difficult author or an agent-hopper.

Code Makers

The codes of ethics for the Independent Literary Agents Association and the Society of Authors' Representatives (see Appendix C) set reasonable standards of conduct for agents whether or not they are members of either group. If your agent is a member of either organization and crosses the line, contact the group (the addresses are given in Chapter 4). The ethics committee may be able to help resolve the situation.

The Light at the End of the Tunnel

Start looking for a new agent the moment you have given your first agent notice that you're leaving. Waiting until you've found a new agent to notify the first one can be embarrassing and create problems for both of them and for you. That's why some agents won't talk to you until you've severed your previous connection. For instance, what if your first agent gets you an offer for a book and you've just signed an agreement with a second one to handle it?

If your agent gives you a good reason to leave, do what will be best for you personally or professionally. Don't be too concerned about being cut adrift in the literary world. It will be easier to find your second agent than it was to find your first one. However, it's not fair to shop around for a new agent while the first one is still working on your behalf.

Agents expect to lose some clients, either because they screw up, fail to sell a book, a book is wildly successful, there's no chemistry, the writer is getting a divorce and wants to shed an agent associated with an unhappy past, or the writer acquires a new spouse who doesn't like the agent. The reasons for firing agents—both valid and inexcusable—are endless. Hollywood agent Marvin Moss thinks that agents should expect to lose 10 percent of their clients a year if only because they stop writing or start writing something the agents don't handle.

Every agent who's been in business a while has been contacted by writers unhappy with their present agents. That you have gotten an agent to take you on lends credibility to you as a writer. If you've had a book published, it will be still easier to find a new agent.

Inalienable Rights

Whomever you choose, however the agent operates, and whether your agreement with your agent is written or oral, both of you have "certain inalienable rights."

A Writer's Bill of Rights

1. As long as your expectations are realistic, you have a right to be

satisfied with everything that happens to your work.

2. You have the right to approve your agent's activities on your behalf.
3. You have the right to expect professionalism in your agent's dealings with publishers and with you.
4. You have the right to see all correspondence written or received about your work.
5. If your agent declines to handle a project, you have the right to sell it or hire another agent to sell it.
6. When your agent has tried all likely publishers for your book, you have the right to take the project back and try to sell it yourself or through another agent.
7. You have the right to be informed promptly about all offers for and helpful responses to your work.
8. You have the right to receive prompt replies to your letters and phone calls.
9. You have the right to understand and approve agreements negotiated on your behalf.
10. You have the right to receive money due you promptly.
11. You have the right to have your business affairs kept confidential.
12. As long as you don't abuse your agent's time, you have the right to ask your agent for news, sympathy, and encouragement.
13. You have the right to ask for reasonable changes in your agency agreement at any time.
14. You have the right to stop working with an agent who is not representing you to your satisfaction.
15. If you end your relationship with your agent, you have the right to receive your work back, with rejection letters.

With rights come responsibilities. As you maintain and improve your relationship with your agent, please keep your obligations to him or her in mind.

An Agent's Bill of Rights

1. Your agent has the right to work however he or she wishes.
2. Your agent has the right to expect the same degree of professionalism from you that you expect from your agent.
3. Your agent has the right to represent a book that competes with yours, provided that handling the competitive book doesn't lessen the agent's ability to represent your book.
4. If a buyer approaches you about your work or services, only your agent has the right to negotiate on your behalf.
5. Except for work you agree to exclude, your agent has the right to

be the only person to represent all of your work for every commercial use.

6. Your agent has the right to continue trying to place a project as long as the agent is conscientiously trying to do so.

7. Your agent has the right to be spared excessive letters, phone calls, and visits.

8. Your agent has the right to be spared personal requests that are not part of an agent's job.

9. In contracts negotiated for you, your agent has the right to include an agent's clause specifying the commission, the agent's right to receive income and mail for you, and the right to act as agent on your behalf.

10. Your agent has the right not to return commissions.

11. If a problem develops between you and your agent, your agent has the right to discuss it with you and to try to solve it to your mutual satisfaction.

12. Your agent has the right to stop representing you at any time.

13. If your agent does a good job for you, the agent earns the right to keep you as a client.

If the Moccasin Fits

"Help me never to judge another until I have walked two weeks in his moccasins." This Sioux prayer may keep you from making an unnecessary mistake in working with your agent. You hired your agent, the agent works for you, and you have the right to be satisfied with what he or she is doing for you.

But harboring unrealistic expectations or misunderstanding your agent's job could destroy a salvageable marriage. Looking at your relationship from your agent's point of view will help you appreciate an agent's problems and concerns. In the next two chapters, you can try my moccasins on for size.

CHAPTER SEVEN

A Terrible Day in the Life of an Agent

To give you a sense of what an agent's life is like, I present the bad news and the good news.

First the agonies. A terrible day in the life of an agent may include any of the following hassles, a composite day-in-the-strife based on real experiences that have happened to us. They are disguised to protect the guilty (you know who you are!) from well-deserved shame and your humble servant from nuisance suits.

If, as most agents do, you work for yourself, agenting can be isolating. Whether you're in or out of New York, most of your work is done by phone and by mail. There are the writers you represent on one side, the people you sell to on the other, and you in the middle. The people, the phone calls, the paper work, and the details are endless. And if you don't get the infinity of minutiae right, sooner or later they may come back to haunt you and cost you time, money, clients, or embarrassment.

Lower phone rates prompt California agents to call their out-of-state clients and New York editors before eight in the morning, which is before eleven o'clock New York time.

The only editor who isn't on another call, not in yet, or at a meeting on this cold, rainy Monday in January blithely announces that the deal we negotiated last week is still not definite, because it needs the approval of a management committee. Usually an editor gets house approval before making an offer. Now I have to tell the author that the deal he and I both thought was firm still has to be approved.

"What do you mean, you don't feel the vibrations are right for me to represent you?"

I've just spilled my coffee on a manuscript as I grabbed the phone for the first incoming call of the day. It's immediately clear that picking up the receiver was my second blunder. In fact, I am now convinced that my real mistake was getting out of bed.

"Well," she continues with a West Marin airiness, "my moon is rising, and since I was born on the cusp, my astral guide assures me that it would not be good for you to represent me."

What's a star-crossed Capricorn to do? I've been fielding this laid-back Libra's questions for two years while she labored on a how-to so far out I thought it just might be in. Finally, I get to read it, and, shock of shocks, it looks salable. Now, thanks to a rising moon, my hours on the phone and my reading time have come to naught, another fitting portent for a bad day.

One of our coagents in Hollywood calls to report a news flash: a movie one week away from starting production has been scrubbed because of an actors' strike. The project, which took more than a year to nudge this far, is as good as dead.

I get a call from a seething client (in her anger, she sounds more like she's teething than seething) who's had it up to here with the subject of an autobiography on which she's collaborating, and with me for bringing the two of them together.

A minute after I finally put the receiver down, the subject also calls in a royal snit, and complains that the writer smokes too much and is dictatorial about how the book should be written and in her unwillingness to make changes, since she is "the writer." Whose story is it, anyway? she demands to know, thoroughly outraged. It's going to take some heavy three-way palavering to keep this project afloat. I promise both of them I'll get back to them soon, wishing it could be in a decade.

Daily two-foot stacks of mail arrive in at least three installments: UPS, package mail, and everything under two pounds in the mailman's big blue bag. Overnight-mail delivery and messengers may also give our doorbell a workout.

With a dull thud, the mailman deposits today's hefty stack of morning mail, containing twelve queries with sample chapters, eight queries without sample chapters, seven rejects, three manuscripts, two proposals, and the usual clump of media, bills, and letters, including this missive:

Dear Mike:

Just wanted to let you know that a writer friend put me in touch with Crapshoot Books, who bought my book. What do you think of that? Another friend who's studying accounting took care of the contract. Many thanks for your help.

What do you think of that? he asks! During the last four months, I've read this turkey's manuscript, made extensive suggestions for revisions, read a revised version, made further suggestions, read a third version, and sent him our agency agreement.

He never told me that he was submitting his manuscript to a publisher, which he shouldn't have done without at least telling me. Worse yet, he doesn't even sense that he's taken advantage of my time and experience, and there's no chance I'll be compensated.

That he probably hasn't gotten the best editor, publisher, or deal for his book is bitter consolation. An angry letter or phone call will only make the situation worse for both of us. All I can do is write the situation off, in the hope that Lady Luck knows that she owes me one.

The next call comes from a weeping, frustrated author on the road who has set herself up an excellent schedule of media appearances (it was too modest a book for the publisher to bother), only to find that the books haven't arrived in town yet, not even in the bookstore where the author is having an autograph party at noon that day.

After a dose of verbal TLC and a successful attempt to find an alternative source of books for the author to sign, my client is once again ready to smile and continue the struggle up the mountain.

The mail isn't finished with me yet. A note from an editor brings news of this disaster: a beautiful art book I was looking forward to seeing has been doomed by a typhoon. How can a typhoon destroy a book? you may ask. Easy, when it's an art book being printed in Hong Kong. The two-week delay in printing and shipping the book means that the book won't reach the stores in time for the Christmas rush, dashing its prospects as a gift book, the basic market for art books. Another book on the slippery slope to Remainder City.

For the first time, we have an author who seems bent on hounding us to death. She finds some inconsequential matter that she regards as sufficient reason to badger us at least once or twice a week. When it finally comes time to negotiate a contract, she isn't satisfied with our efforts on her behalf, so she makes her own calls to the editor! The poor editor is already not looking forward to working with the writer.

The contract is now signed, and we will represent her for the project, but to save my sanity, I am sending her a letter giving her sixty days' notice, after which we will no longer represent her on future projects. She's definitely a writer who's better off representing herself.

Still more gloom from the mail pouch: our agency agreement allows clients to end the agreement with sixty days' notice by registered mail. Signing for a registered letter from a client always causes an uneasy anticipation that is usually fulfilled by a writer's saying good-bye.

Today is no exception. We tried for three years to sell a science fiction novel for a guy in Montana and finally succeeded, beyond our expectations, because the editor who bought it wanted a series. The series didn't make the author rich, and he decided that his career wasn't moving far enough, fast enough, and it was our fault.

Having opted to take lunch at my desk to stay dry and catch up with the mounting piles of printed matter, I open the next letter bomb as I try to consume a soggy tuna-fish sandwich on cold toast. An editor is rejecting the finished manuscript of a specialized how-to book that took twenty-three submissions and a year and a half to sell and is unlikely to be sold elsewhere. The reason: Her publishing house has been gobbled up by a larger one with no interest in the subject. The excuse the editor is forced to use is that the illustrations are late.

And while there's a chance that we could cajole the house into doing the book, they would undoubtedly kill it with indifference. I am left with the joyless task of informing the author.

I stab myself with a staple as I open a jiffy bag sealed with twenty staples instead of the five it requires.

The mail does bring a check. That's good news. The bad news is that the check came about because the numbers on an author's royalty statement made us holler, "Tilt!" and we're still wondering if the author got all the royalties due him.

I place a call to the last of ten editors considering a multiple submission, and learn that the manuscript is on its way back. It's a how-to book I'm very excited about, and even editors are returning the project with the kind of glowing rejections you could frame, but they just can't get the clods in marketing to agree.

As an agent, you encounter your share of crazies. William Targ, a publisher and former editor, who bought Mario Puzo's *The Godfather* for $5,000 after two editors had turned it down, once remarked: "The trouble with the publishing business is that too many people who have half a mind to write a book do so." He must have been thinking of these folks.

Their ideas are bizarre, their writing unredeemable, and they are most anxious to impart a limitless supply of useless information about the project before you even have a chance to read it. You are stuck between not wanting to have anything to do with them and not wanting to risk offending them. All you can do is suffer quietly and break off contact with them as quickly and gracefully as you can manage, which I do with the latest caller from another planet.

Near the end of the day, I have the depressing task of calling one of our Hollywood agents to let her know that our client has made his choice between the two offers for his book. One was for a small but fair sum from an earnest young producer with no credits; the other for twice as much money from an Oscar-winning director. Our client chose earnestness, which cost him and us money and cost the project the services and credibility of a proven director. Melancholy proof that to a degree, agents can be only as effective as clients let them.

The only merciful thing about this day is that it finally ends, leaving me wondering what artfully concealed streak of masochism chains me to this painfully depressing way of slow death. Why do I let myself continue to be abused by selfish writers, crass editors, no-talent strangers, and lousy luck?

It took five years to start making a living as an agent, and I spent part of that time driving a taxi to pay the rent. I've been in the business more than a decade now, and sometimes I think that becoming an agent was the worst mistake of my life.

Lord knows, I'm not doing it because of publishers' royalties or authors' loyalties. Most books don't even earn out their advances. And writers usually don't appreciate what you do for them. No matter how hard you work for them, if something goes wrong, even if it's not your fault, or if they suddenly strike it rich, William Morris, here they come! And the work is never finished. There is always another, most likely unsalable, manuscript to read and reject. Who needs it?

My day ends, as most days do, by reading a succession of queries and proposals, all of which have only one virtue: They fail to keep me awake.

For agents, especially those who, like us, work out of their homes, not even an answering machine can spare one from phone calls at midnight, and on weekends and holidays, including Christmas, from budding geniuses who have just finished masterpieces and assume that you're sitting by the phone waiting for their calls.

So to top off this terrible day, the phone wakes me up at five minutes to twelve. It'a guy who, judging from the background noise, is in a bar and sounds utterly sloshed. He wants to know if I would be interested in seeing a best-selling novel he is thinking (!) of writing.

I force myself to tell him politely that he should call back between nine and five. He insists on rambling on. Finally, I lose patience, he gets abusive, and the call ends abruptly and unhappily for both of us.

I decide to take a stab at just one more manuscript to try to salvage something from what has been a thoroughly miserable day. Numbed by the inadequacy of what I have endured so far, I start reading . . .

CHAPTER EIGHT

A Terrific Day in the Life of an Agent

. . . a first novel in the form of letters from a seven-year-old boy to Superman. Is he kidding? I think at first. How is he going to bring off a 210-page novel (I always check page length) out of a kid's letters?

But by page 20 I'm hooked. And by the end of the book, he has made me laugh and cry by using the simplicity of a child's letters to provide insight into sex, God, religion, innocence, love, family, school, growing up, and small-town life. It's a timeless, universal, enthralling novel that will appeal to kids as well as grownups.

As I read it, it gives me chills to know I am discovering a major new talent. Also while I read, names of editors who will be right for the book spring to mind unbidden (agents will understand this phenomenon). When I finish the manuscript, I can't wait to share it with Elizabeth and meet the author. (After the book is published, the American Library Association selects it as one of the best books of the year for young adults.)

The discovery of this manuscript in the wee hours of the morning is only the start of a perfect day-in-the-life.

It's a glorious spring morning. The sky is clear, the air is crisp, and the sun is turning new leaves brilliant green, one of my favorite colors. After I finish my morning walk in a park nearby, I pick up the paper on my way home and find an excellent review of one of our books, a sign of glad tidings to come.

Agenting is a great business for optimists. The day's reading, mail, meetings, and phone calls may yield—
- An irresistibly moving, inspiring, and commercial book
- A book that will change the world, or at least improve it
- Checks, large and small, for domestic and foreign sales; especially welcome are the checks you aren't expecting and those that are larger than you were expecting
- A letter from a new writer or editor who turns out to be a wonderful human being as well as a first-rate professional

- Calls from new writers who say that an author, agent, editor, bookseller, or reviewer we admire recommended the agency
- A contract negotiation in which we obtain at least some degree of satisfaction on all of the changes we request
- An offer for a book that exceeds our expectations, from a good new publisher
- News of a first-serial, foreign, movie, book-club, or a six-figure paperback reprint sale
- A meeting with a writer who has rewritten a proposal exactly as I requested and that I feel certain I'll be able to sell

Our English agent calls to announce that he has just sold the English rights to a novel before pub date. The author is so pleased that he brings over a bottle of Dom Perignon to celebrate.

An editor calls to wrap up a two-day auction that, with escalators, winds up in six figures. I call the author two thousand miles away, and he reports that work on his next book is proceeding beautifully.

"You know," he says, "what's the best thing you and Elizabeth have done for me?"

"What?" I ask, wondering.

"Your success with my books has given me the freedom to write without having to worry about the rent, and that's the greatest gift you could have given me. I just want you to know that I really appreciate all that you've done for me."

I am delighted that we've helped free him to write, and the kindness of his words makes me misty-eyed. It was a short speech, but I have heard it only once, and it's Mozart to my ears. Those are sweet words for an agent to hear. He just made my day.

Nor do I deceive myself into taking an undue share of the credit. His willingness to endure rejections and hang on for four years until his work gained in popularity, and most of all his ability to write, are what won him his freedom. My getting his books to a receptive editor and publisher helped, but ultimately it was book buyers responding to his gifts as a storyteller who freed him to write.

Agents thrive on a fascinating paradox: Every day is the same and every day is different. You do the same kinds of things, but each project is a challenge, because it involves a unique combination of subject, author, publisher, and timing.

The many projects with which you're involved are in different stages of development. And there's a constant stream of new ideas and people whizzing by hoping to interest you. If you are excited by new ideas, it's impossible to stagnate or become bored. The years fly by.

If, as most agents do, you work for yourself, you have the freedom to set your ethical standards and operating procedures as you see fit, and as soon as your income allows, you can handle only books you feel strongly about and refuse the rest.

Another one of our favorite authors calls. She fulfilled many a Midwest housewife's dream by plunking her typewriter down on her kitchen table and turning out her first historical novel. With six books already in a series, she's still writing up a storm. She's a warm, delightful lady, and it's always a pleasure to hear how she's coming along on her next opus.

The mail brings a two-book contract from a hot new publisher. The covering letter includes the following paragraph:

> *It is a pleasure to do business with you. The proposals you have provided for my consideration are polished and comprehensive. Your expertise in preparing authors for the publishing process has facilitated my decision making and acquisitions activity. Additionally, a number of the proposals you represent have very stong market potential. I look forward to our continued communications.*

Today's UPS delivery includes an advance copy of a book just off the press. The jacket looks super, and I open the book and see this:

"Words would get in the way were I to try to articulate what I feel for Elizabeth Pomada and Michael Larsen who have become much, much more than my agents."

When a writer cares enough about the editorial help you've provided and the two and a half years you've spent selling the book, sustained only by your friendship and conviction, to preface the book like that, you know that, regardless of how well the book does, it was time well spent.

Fortunately, this book became a best seller, and there are few greater joys in life for either a writer or an agent than seeing your first book on *The New York Times* best-seller list. It justifies your faith in the book, the author, and the publisher's ability to make it work. You bask in the satisfaction of knowing that across the country, thousands of readers are enjoying the book and telling their friends about it, creating a word-of-mouth snowball effect, still the most effective way to promote a book.

Now it's time to meet one of the best editors in the business for one of those long, legendary literary lunches writers hear about. Despite the three-martini tradition, Perrier and white wine are the potables of choice. We both have an afternoon's work ahead of us.

An editor with his own imprint who has headed West for a writer's conference, he has been responsible for many literary as well as commercial successes. His passion for books and publishing remains undiminished even after enough years in the business to turn his temples gray.

By the end of lunch, I feel exhilarated. Once again, I know that despite the hard knocks, the book business is the only way to make a living.

On the basis of what she called "the best proposal I've ever seen," a hard-cover editor made a substantial offer for a book. She rides home on the train with a mass-market editor. When I get back from lunch, she calls gleefully to let us know that, six weeks before the book is going to be published, the mass-market editor is so excited about the book that she has made an opening $50,000 offer for the paperback rights.

The mail brings the latest issue of *Publishers Weekly*, which has a very effective ad for one of our books on the cover, the opening shot of a $50,000 promotional campaign.

One of our authors presents seminars on entrepreneuring. I attended one of them and received a list of 555 ways to earn extra money. I took it home, and the next day, I thought to myself: "That's a book!" And sure enough, less than two years later, it was. On the Acknowledgments page, the author thanked "my high-determination, high-imagination literary agent . . . the person who suggested the book to me in the first place, then coaxed and coddled it to its place in your hands."

I don't include these kind words to pat myself on the back. This kind of recognition is one of the joys of an agent's life, and will be greatly appreciated by your agent. Only a handful of us get rich from the job, so, like writers, the rest need all the psychic rewards we can get.

The widow of an author calls after receiving a small royalty check to thank us again for getting her husband's work republished. The book came out twenty years ago, got rave reviews, and then went OP (out of print). Since the book held up so well, we were able to place it with a university press that does a series of lost American fiction and is allied with a mass-market house, which means that the book had a new paperback edition. We were pleased that books of enduring value have a way of surviving neglect.

A call comes from the last of fourteen editors to read what we think is an American classic. She agrees, and is determined to get the book the recognition it deserves. When an editor calls and tells you that a manuscript that has been around the block is an American classic, and you've been waiting for more than a year to hear those words, you know you've finally found a niche for the book on the right list.

Finding an editor who loves a book as much as you do is guaranteed to send chills up and down your spine. And the editor backs up her feelings with a solid advance, along with advertising and first-printing commitments. That's my kind of phone call!

Our evening's festivities begin when one of our authors, who has written a book about her adventures as a commercial fisherwoman, arrives with a thirty-pound albacore tuna! She takes one look at our combination of delight and chagrin and, bless her heart, decides that she'd better clean it for us. We feast on the freshest sashimi we've ever tasted.

One of our writers is an artist who writes six days a week and settles for nothing less than the best work of which he is capable. His combination of talent, vision, and devotion makes him one of America's most promising writers. When he writes, he is forging literary links with the future that will outlive us all. During dinner, the main course being the pleasure of his company, his desire to promote his books and his dedication to writing for posterity as well as for a living illuminate our lives and make for an inspiring evening. He is a friend as well as a client. What wonders, we ask ourselves, will he be creating in ten years?

At the end of the day, we go to a sneak preview of a comedy made from one of our books. It's wildly funny, if mildly off-color in spots, but that may add to its appeal.

The author lives out of town, so, unlike the other patrons in the theater, you won't be surprised to learn that we are the only people in the place who cheer during the titles when the phrase "Based on the novel by . . ." flashes on the screen.

My faith in the value of life and books restored, it's home to hit the manuscript pile again, hoping to find another artist before sleep overtakes me. Yes, agenting is a great business for optimists. Diane Cleaver, author of *The Literary Agent and the Writer: A Professional Guide*, once called it "the perfect profession." Well, it may not be perfect, but it will do until someone invents something better.

CHAPTER NINE

The Brave New Whirl: Publishing at a Passage

"If we want things to stay as they are, things will have to change." — The Leopard, the beautiful, best-selling novel by Giuseppe di Lampedusa, published posthumously because the only publisher to whom the author sent it turned it down.

When RCA bought Random House (which it has since sold to the Newhouse newspaper empire), the accountants were going over Random House's books. At one point, one of them looked up from a ledger with a sudden sense of revelation and exclaimed: "Hey! I got a great idea! Let's just publish the best sellers!"

Ned Leavitt, an agent at William Morris, has observed that agents' aptitudes and inclinations lie somewhere between those who are editorially oriented and those who are deal-oriented, those primarily interested in words and those primarily interested in dollar signs. Ideally, an agent should be a happy medium between these two extremes.

This tension between mammon and the muse is inextricably linked to what winds up between covers. As you and your agent set out on the adventure of getting your book published, you should have an understanding of the book business and the working conditions of an editor, who, after your agent, will be your closest ally.

Like the rest of the arts, publishing must tread the tightrope between art and commerce. Like writers and agents, publishers want to sell their books with pride and passion, but to survive, they must have books that sell.

This fundamental dilemma of the publishing business is captured perfectly by a cartoon in *Writer's Digest* in which an editor reassures an eager young writer by saying: "This a sensitive, beautifully written story, Ms. Bentley, but don't worry, I'm sure our editors can turn it into a salable property."

Major houses have an appetite for both popcorn and caviar. They want classy books but are not above publishing the commercial books that help support them. An executive vice-president of marketing at Simon & Schuster, once explained why: "There are three reasons to publish a book: It will make a profit; the subject is so important it has to be published; or the author shows promise. Without a profit, you can't do the other two."

Passage to the Future

In *Passages*, Gail Sheehy's best seller about personal development, periods of struggle and uncertainty are passages we must endure as we progress from one stage of life to the next. Right now, publishing is making its way through a passage. Prodded by costs, computers, conglomerates, and competition, it is changing faster and more radically than at any time since it began in England two hundred years ago.

This passage will be crucial in shaping the future of American publishing. What is evolving in the areas of management, distribution, manufacturing, rising costs, word processing, electronic media, the growing concentration of publishers and booksellers, discounting, censorship, copyright, and First-Amendment rights will affect authors and publishing in a profound, irreversible way.

You should be aware of the trends and realities that affect you, your agent, and your publisher, and maintain a positive but realistic perspective on the book business. First the realities:

• In round numbers, as of this writing, America's 20,000 publishers unleash 50,000 books a year and generate sales of $11,000,000,000 annually from the 700,000 titles in print. These include trade, mass market, religious, professional, mail-order, and university-press books; textbooks; subscription reference series; books sold through book clubs; and new editions of previously published books.

• Retail sales in the country's 10,000 bookstores and the 100,000 outlets that carry mass-market books account for less than half of industry sales. While these numbers may be impressive, they represent only a tiny part of the American economy.

• Publishing a book is a personal, complex, collective enterprise. To have the best chance for success, your book should be well edited, designed, produced, sold by the sales reps and the subsidiary-rights departments, distributed, promoted, reviewed, and stocked by booksellers. A multitude of things can go wrong during the publication of a book, and some will. To publish a book perfectly is practically impossible.

To worsen the problem, too many books are published to receive the attention they require from publishers, booksellers, reviewers, or book buyers. Distribution, getting books into stores and keeping them there, is the industry's greatest weakness. Because booksellers can return unsold books, returns are a perpetual migraine for which publishers have yet to find a cure.

To get a feeling for the endless flow of books into which yours will merge, browse in bookstores. Ask booksellers about what's selling. Look at the most recent announcement issue (February and August) of *Publishers Weekly* in your library.

• Most hard-cover publishers have spring and fall lists of books; mass-market houses have monthly ones. After publishers' sales conferences in May and December to sell their representatives on new lists (and they are a tough sell!), the reps fan out across the country hawking their wares. Consequently, major New York publishers want books of national interest.

Where luck plays a hand is in finding the right editor at the right house at the right time. This is because, in addition to the three ingredients your book needs to be successful—the best possible editor, publisher, and deal—your book must be published at the right time. Timing is the fourth essential ingredient in a book's success.

Bob Levine, the former Editor in Chief of a small New York house, once remarked: "The more I know, the less I know." Like writers and agents, publishers are dancing in the dark, guessing what book buyers want to read, how much a book is worth, and how best to publish it.

One of the most frustrating publishing truths is that regardless of how much or little a publisher spends to buy or promote a book, it is usually impossible to predict how the book will do.

Sometimes, all you need is luck. Here is how the unexpected success of a low-budget rock film resulted in a best seller. In the spring of 1978, disco dancing exploded in popularity, but word had not yet percolated up to the Big Apple's editorial boardrooms. True to the California tradition of being ahead of its time, Karen Lustgarten's proposal for a disco book had been circulating for over a year with no takers.

It wasn't us who finally sold the book, it was John Travolta. A front-page story in *The New York Times* certified the phenomenon caused by *Saturday Night Fever* and the opening of disco-dance palaces around the country. In two weeks, we placed the book. Warner put it on a crash schedule, sent Karen on a national tour as part of a $50,000 promotion campaign, and *The Complete Guide to Disco Dancing* coasted for almost three months on the *Times* best-seller list.

• By the time your book is written, sold, and then produced and distributed by a large house, one and a half to two years will usually pass. Publishers like to jump on bandwagons, but not too early or too late, or they land on their financial keisters. When everybody jumps, the result is bookicide: Too many publishers pounce on a hot subject and suffocate it with a barrage of similar books. The short-lived computer-book boom in the early 1980s is a costly example of the phenomenon.

Three Against the House

• Your agent is a matchmaker who tries to arrange a working marriage between you and the best editor for your work. What are editors? They are publishers, specialists, visionaries, in-house agents, conspirators, the ultimate middlemen and -women, and, according to *San Francisco Chronicle* Book Review Editor Pat Holt, the heroes of the business.

Marc Jaffe, who has his own imprint at Houghton Mifflin, once remarked: "A competent editor is a publisher in microcosm, able to initiate and follow a project all the way through." Editors are intrapreneurs—entrepreneurs within organizations—each with his or her own invisible imprint. Like the publishers for whom they work, they rise and fall on the strength of their decisions. If they don't help fill in the black side of the ledger, they will have to find another house to set up shop in.

While some editors are generalists who will consider anything their houses can publish successfully, most editors have a range of fiction and nonfiction specialties that blends with the house's needs and their own passions. An editor may prefer contemporary, historical, literary, or commercial fiction. Usually there will be an editor responsible for acquiring books on specialized subjects like sports, cooking, dance, fitness, child care.

Editors are visionaries. They see not just what a book is, but what it could be. An editor's most valuable gift is the ability to reconcile the writer's vision with the reader's needs, to discern the ideal way to present a writer's ideas as well as to inspire a writer's best work. Dick Marek, Dutton president, feels that since the writer is subjective, the editor must be objective, to draw out the writer's best work.

The French writer André Maurois once quipped: "In literature, as in love, we are astonished at what is chosen by others." Art, like life, is a Rorschach. That's why we've sold books to the third editor at a house to read them. But editors see only what they're ready to see. Like the rest of us, editors have their own biases, intuitions, and idiosyncrasies. So even if editors' tastes predispose them to like your manuscript, if they're feeling grumpy when they read it, they still may not be receptive to it.

Editors may have assistants who screen manuscripts for them, creating another potential barrier for your manuscript. Editors, like agents, reject over 90 percent of what they see. But once an editor likes your book, you no longer have one agent, you have two.

Your editor is your in-house agent. Even if an editor adores your book, that's only the first hurdle. Your editor then shares your manuscript with other editors and other likely allies, to gather support for it. At most major houses, editors have to fill out a lengthy proposal-to-publish form, describing a book's costs, contents, and markets, and sales, subsidiary-rights, and promotion potential.

The quintessential editorial response is: "I see it. I love it. I publish it." But editors must justify their enthusiasm to an editorial board that will include other editors, members of the sales, publicity, and subsidiary-rights departments, and executives of the company, all of whom function as devil's advocates for the house. If any one of them can come up with a reason that seems to justify not doing a book, they'll pass on it and go on to the next book. Subjectivity and the group grope for the right decision are two of the reasons why editors turn down manuscripts that become best sellers.

If your book is bought, you, your agent, and your editor are united in a conspiracy to publish your book as successfully as possible. No one else in the house will know or care as much about your book as the three of you. So despite whatever resistance and competition stand in your book's way, you must stick together when problems arise.

Editors are the ultimate middlemen. They have to deal with authors, agents, other editors, subsidiary-rights people, sales reps and other marketing people, publicists, the advertising department, the art director, production people, and company officers on every one of their books. They also represent readers. At hard-cover houses, an editor may do fifteen to twenty-five books a year.

Editors write the copy for the catalog and the jacket. But an editor may spend so much time in meetings and in acquiring books that the actual editing of a manuscript may be left to an assistant or a free-lancer.

Editors tend to be overworked and underpaid. It's been estimated that wage slaves in the corporate world have no more than six minutes at a stretch to work before they are interrupted by a meeting or a phone call. Editors can't read submissions during the day; they read them at night, on weekends, and on vacation. And unless they are interested in buying a book, they won't take the time to think about how a submission might be improved to make it work. All they do is say yes or no as quickly as they can and move to the next manuscript on the bottomless pile. In fact, the perfect title for an editor's autobiography would be *Piles to Go Before I Sleep*.

An editor once told us that in the course of buying, editing, and proofing a manuscript, he read every book he bought at least seven times. One writer who sent us a manuscript admitted that he hadn't even read it once! He just typed it up and shipped it out!

Jim Landis, who has his own imprint at William Morrow, figures that it takes him twenty minutes to edit a page. Multiply that by 200 and you will see how much time it takes to edit a book well.

Your editor may be as important as your publisher in determining the fate of your book. Editors who take the time to edit, who inspire the writers they work with, and who are passionate advocates for their books at every stage of publication deserve to be regarded as the heroes of the business.

Lunging for the Brass Ring

• Like agents and publishers, books tend to come in two sizes: big and small, best sellers and everything else. During its ride on the publishing merry-go-round, a book has six lunges to grab the brass ring of best-sellerdom.

Every hard-cover house hopes to parlay the momentum generated by

- A big advance
- In-house enthusiasm
- A rave review in *Publishers Weekly*
- Huge first-serial, movie, paperback, and book club sales
- A front-page review in *The New York Times*
- And an effective promotion campaign with a promotable author into a tidal wave of glowing word-of-mouth recommendations on which a book will sail to the top of the best-seller lists.

When *PW* took a poll about why people read, they found that the most important reason is pleasure: first the pleasure of reading the book, then the pleasure of touting it to friends. That's why word of mouth alone can make a book despite the indifference with which it is ushered into the world.

The first four of these lunges are prenatal influences which occur before publication. If a book is sinking in still water when pub date rolls around, the editor and the rest of the house will be too busy thinking about the next list to pay attention to it. Its fate will be decided by the reception the first printing receives from reviewers and book buyers. Small wonder, then, that nearly 80 percent of the books published lose money.

Without including the advance and the cost of printing books, the average investment a major publisher makes in a book is more than fifty thousand dollars. Holding down advances and royalties and trying to retain rights usually withheld for authors are three methods publishers employ to ease their burden. Because hard-cover houses can no longer count on large reprint sales to paperback houses, they don't want to rely on subsidiary-rights sales to justify buying a book. They want all of their books to pull their own weight.

Looking Out for the Competition

• Another inescapable reality is the competition your book faces. The competition starts with you. The idea for your book may be in competition with other ideas for your time and energy. Writing and promoting the book may compete with your other priorities.

Before it is taken on, your project will be in competition with every idea, proposal, manuscript, and book that agents and editors have read, heard about, accepted, and rejected.

After it is accepted, your book will compete with every other book your agent, your editor, your publicist, the sales reps, and the production and subsidiary rights departments are responsible for.

The book will also compete with your publisher's other books for promotional resources.

After publication, your book will compete with all of the books on your publisher's backlist, especially those on the same subject.

Your book will compete with all of the books in print on the same subject.

Your book will be in competition for time and space with all of the products, services, and causes, and people seeking publicity.

The book will compete for the attention of reviewers: About 20,000 trade books are published every year. *The New York Times* reviews only about one-tenth of them.

Distributors and booksellers can't stock all of the books that are published. The business of chain stores is predicated upon volume, so they rely on best-sellers, hot topics, gimmick books, and remainders—publishers' overstock they can buy cheaply—to keep their cash registers ringing.

Independent booksellers who lack the chains' advantages of higher discounts and promotional allowances must be extremely careful about the kind and the quantity of books they order.

There are always more candidates for book-club, movie, paperback reprint, foreign, and other subsidiary rights sales than there are takers. For example, the Book of the Month Club considers 6,000 books a year, but selects just 5 percent of them, only 300 books a year. As much as writers want to think so, books are not a basic necessity like food, clothing, and shelter. They are purchased with "discretionary income," whatever is left over after the basics are paid for. What media will your book be in competition with for consumers' spare time and money? Television, movies, newspapers and magazines, audio and video cassettes, and software. Most of these media are comparably priced or less. They are all easier to enjoy, faster to finish, and more superficially exciting than books.

Your book will suffer from the growing problem of illiteracy. In his moving book, *Illiterate America*, Jonathan Kozol argues that one-third of the country's adults—60 million people—can't read the front page of a newspaper. This number grows by 10 percent every year. Millions more are *aliterate*; they *can* read but *don't*.

This list wasn't meant to discourage you but to make you aware of the complex cultural landscape in which you are trying to find a home for your books. Consider this: With the right book and the right agent, the media that compete *with* your book can be sources of income *from* it.

To Be or OP

As publishers plunge headlong into the future, these trends are worth noting.

• I once saw a cartoon in which a bookseller looks up from a copy of *Books in Print* and informs a customer in search of a book: "I'm sorry, sir, but *The Future of Publishing* is out of print."

Although, as Chronicle Books sales rep Carla Ruff once quipped, "No one is ever going to curl up with a floppy disk," computers are transforming the way books are written, edited, manufactured, sold, and used. They are also creating markets both for books about the new technology and for new electronic media such as software and databases.

• In what may be a cyclical, century-old pattern, the urge to merge caused a mergermania in publishing that began in the sixties and has created a two-tier industry. The appearance of conglomerates on the publishing scene has produced a winner-take-all glamour industry with better financing, and more effective marketing and management. But they have also led to minimizing risk, overproduction, the emergence of communications conglomerates forming a Hollywood-TV-publishing complex, and a shotgun marketing approach: Fire enough literary salvos at the public and you're bound to hit a few bull's-eyes.

The apex of the publishing pyramid is inhabited by the symbiotic mega tribe who worship the bottom line and look to the star system for their salvation.

The tribe must have a continuous supply of megabooks which are sold on the basis of micro-outlines to the dozen megapublishers who capitulate to the megabuck demands of mega-agents and their mega-star clients whose only loyalty is to the highest bidder. The tribe's mating rituals are performed at the choicest soirees and the "in" restaurants where the elite meet to eat.

In a megadeal, a book's hard cover, paperback, book-club, film, foreign-rights, serialization, and promotion potential are parts of a media megapackage which is carefully orchestrated for maximum impact. For the mega tribe, maximum impact means two things: being Number One and extracting as much profit from the other members of the tribe as possible.

This is the age of heavily discounted mass-market hard cover, the million-copy-selling blockbusters like James Michener's novels and *Iacocca: An Autobiography*. Reduced overhead and economics of scale make it more profitable for publishers to sell 100,000 copies of one book than 10,000 copies of ten books. And the advances lavished on the megastars leave less money for new writers who need it more, but must rely on psychic income instead.

However at the base of the publishing pyramid, computer technology, enterprising writers and publishers, and the censorship of the marketplace have created more than 18,000 small presses and self-publishers, a flourishing cottage industry which has sprung up to develop new writers and new ideas.

In between the large and the small publishers are the medium-sized houses who carry on without benefit either of the resources of the megapublishers or the low overhead of the small presses.

Nonprofit university presses are also filling the publishing vacuum for less commercial midlist books by becoming more trade-oriented.

The growing concentration of publishers and booksellers raises the stakes of the publishing gamble, making it harder for new writers to break into the business with a major publisher.

• What are publishers buying? Three kinds of fiction predominate:

1. Genre books, such as mysteries, westerns, romances, and science fiction
2. Literary novels, on which hardcover houses are reluctant to lose money while waiting for a writer to give birth to a best seller, but which have found new life as paperback originals
3. Best sellers, which may be genre books with enough heft, scope, and storytelling ability; literary novels; or commercial blockbusters

All houses want best sellers, and large publishers in the heat of an auction bid seven figures for them. If publishers believe they're wagering on the next Robert Ludlum or Judith Krantz, they're eager to bet a bundle in the best-seller sweepstakes.

Fiction, more than nonfiction, is a brand-name business. Once authors have paid their dues to join the best-seller club by writing several novels you never heard of and write their "breakthrough" novels, they have a good shot at a lifetime membership. Most of the novels on the best-seller list are by members of the best-seller club.

Beyond the value of the authors themselves, best sellers are important to publishers because they lead the rest of a publisher's list into the bookstores. At mass-market houses, the top books are called "leaders."

In nonfiction, publishers will do almost anything for the general public that will sell in bookstores and that ideally has other markets such as schools and libraries. Nonfiction runs the gamut. There are front-list humor and novelty books that make a splash, then disappear.

At the other extreme is the philosophy of annuity publishing; that is, solid how-tos and biographies, backlist books, which go on selling year after year.

• Packaging a book, that is, providing a publisher with a complete copy-edited manuscript, a camera-ready version of the text and artwork, or finished books has created a new breed of publishing entrepreneuer, the packager or book producer. Usually former editors, they generate ideas, sell them with proposals, and use a network of freelancers to deliver the project. Editors find packagers especially helpful with illustrated books requiring a lot of production work, since packagers can finish a book faster and cheaper than a publisher.

Because of the ability to use computers for typesetting and the availability of short-run printing, thousands of authors are becoming self-publishers.

- There are more formats for your book to appear in than ever before:
    - It can be a hard cover. The price and relative sturdiness of hard covers make them principally an information medium, the format for books with lasting value one wants to keep for reference.
    - It can be a mass-market or rack-size book that fits into the wire racks you find in supermarkets, airports, and drugstores. The opening salvo of America's Paperback Revolution was fired in 1939 when Pocket Books published ten 25-cent mass-market paperbacks. In contrast to hard-cover books, the mass-market book has for the most part been an entertainment medium, providing classics, genre novels, and best sellers for readers in search of escape.
    - It can be a trade paperback in any size from a Garfield cartoon book to *The Whole Earth Catalog*. The Anchor Books imprint at Doubleday, started in 1953, is regarded as the starting point in the history of trade paperbacks, making it the newest of the three formats.

        Trade paperbacks are sold primarily in bookstores. While costing only about a dollar less to manufacture, they are priced lower than hard covers. The lower price means that authors receive lower royalties and publishers must sell several times as many copies for the authors to earn the equivalent of the hard cover income.

        Price and the variety of formats and sizes make trade paperbacks the all purpose medium, suitable for words and pictures, fiction and nonfiction, the serious and the frivolous, for stores and for course adoptions, for reference and for gifts. Rising prices are making paperbacks the mainstay of trade publishing.

It can be any combination of these formats, or even all three simultaneously. A publisher will do a book in whatever format works best. Since several large houses do all three, they can control the timing and marketing of each edition.

The great benefit to you from such flexibility is this: When a hardcover house sells the paperback rights to a book, the income is split between the author and the publisher. If your publisher does both editions or your hard-cover publisher goes into partnership at the outset with another house for the paperback, you receive full royalties.

• As if in pursuit of futurist John Naisbitt's dream of world peace through world trade, the internationalization of publishing is accelerating. Two signs: the growing foreign presence at the American Booksellers Convention and the merging of American and European publishers.

• According to the doomsday prophets, the bicycle, the car, the radio, movies, television, and the computer were all supposed to sound the death knell for books. But books survived, and are reused more than any of the other media.

One day you will be able to order and receive books on your computer. But even then, as an affordable, efficient, portable, lasting, and sometimes beautiful means of communication, books will remain part of the media mix.

• While New York will remain the center of publishing, the book business is spreading out. There are more writers, agents, publishers, booksellers, and book buyers in more places than ever.

To keep up with news about writing and publishing, read *Coda*, *Writer's Digest*, *The Writer*, *Publishers Weekly*, and at least the book review section of *The New York Times*, and, as Chapter 4 recommends, develop your professional network.

The writing and publishing of your book will be a rite of passage for you. You will go from being someone who thinks you can write a book and have a salable idea to being an author, a potentially life-changing experience. To make the most of it, venture forth armed with a clear but motivating vision of the brave new whirl you're entering.

CHAPTER TEN

The Book Contract: Tiptoeing Through a Diamond-Studded Minefield

"The writer, owing to his temperament, his lack of business train-ing, and his frequent isolation from other members of his profession, is especially unfitted to drive a good bargain with those who buy his man-uscripts."
—From a pamphlet issued by the Author's League of America, 1912

"Will you be needing an advance?"
—A contemporary senior editor's advice to colleagues on what to ask prospective authors after lunch. Why?
"You'd be surprised how often they say no."

"You know that book we spoke about last week? Well, I brought it up at the editorial-board meeting this morning, and got a go-ahead. I'd like to make you an offer for it."

To help you understand what happens after this phone call, here is an agent's perspective on the issues and the process involved in negotiat-ing a contract.

The longer an agent has waited to hear those words, the sweeter they sound. Usually, when an offer is made, the editor has already spoken to the agent to:

- Verify that the book is still available
- Let the agent know that the editor is interested, so that if the book is being considered by other houses, the agent won't accept anoth-er offer without first talking to the editor
- See if any other offers have been made on the book
- Find out what kind of advance the agent is looking for, to make sure that it's in the same ballpark as what the editor is thinking about offering. Just as it's essential for you and your agent to share

the same literary and financial vision of your book, both of you must also agree with the editor's perspective on the book.

* Tell the agent when to expect a phone call about the house's decision

Striking a Deal

When the editor calls back, buoyed by the victory of getting the book through the editorial board and eager to make an offer, the discussion will cover the following topics:

1. Your advance
2. The pay-out: how your advance will be paid
3. Your royalties
4. In a hard-cover contract, how paperback income will be split
5. Rights being withheld for you
6. Issues particular to your book

Depending on how valuable a property you and the book are, and therefore how much clout your agent brings to the negotiations, this first conversation may also take up the issues of:

7. Expense money
8. Advance escalators for appearances on the best-seller list
9. An advance escalator on a movie sale
10. A promotion budget for the book
11. A first-printing guarantee

The editor covers the essential points of the deal, and, depending on the circumstances, may indicate whether there is any flexibility in the numbers. The agent will usually discuss some or all of these points. Then the agent thanks the editor for the offer and promises to get back to the editor after consulting with the author and, again depending on the circumstances, any other publishers who have the project.

A contract is a diamond-studded minefield that divides a finite sum of money between two parties. Since contracts are written by publishers, they are loaded with potentially explosive clauses that contain opportunities for your publisher to profit at your expense.

The more money your publisher keeps, the less you get. Since publishers exist to make a profit, with cultural uplift in most cases a secondary consideration, publishers try to hold on to as much of the money a contract generates as they can.

They do this by trying to hold down advances and royalties, by retaining as many subsidiary rights to a book as they can and maximizing their share of the income from these rights, by trying to tie down the author's next book, and by including in the contract circumstantial clauses that benefit them by lowering the author's income. They can't readily get concessions from their printers or their customers, but for most publishers, an unsuspecting author is always fair game. "Boilerplates," publishers' printed contract forms, run from four to more than twenty-eight pages. Their function, once they're filled in with terms, is to establish a more or less mutually satisfactory business and financial basis for the publication of your book.

A large publisher may have more than one standard contract. I have heard of an editor who keeps three contracts on hand, and whether he's dealing with a new writer, an experienced writer, or an agent determines which one he pulls out of his desk drawer.

The Agent as Hired Haggler

Negotiating with writers puts editors in a schizophrenic position. When it comes to the book itself, editors and writers share an interest in working together as closely as possible to create the best possible book. Editors want to establish continuing relationships with writers. They know that haggling about money or taking advantage of an author's naivete will hurt their chances to do so.

Yet editors are paid by publishers, not by writers, and part of what they get paid to do is buy books as cheaply as possible. Responsible editors know that they will be trying to increase their houses' profits at the expense of writers, so they resolve this dilemma by recommending that writers find an agent. Some editors suggest agents to contact.

When former Knopf Editor-in-Chief Bob Gottlieb accepted Cyra McFadden's best-selling novel, *The Serial*, he suggested that she get an agent and gave her three names. The first two said that they would be glad to represent her without even seeing her book. The third agent, Elaine Markson, wanted to read her novel before deciding. That's what made Cyra choose Elaine as her agent.

Dealing with the Deal Points

The sale of your book will take place or fall through depending on the ability and willingness of your publisher, your agent, and you to agree on what all of you consider a fair deal. Let's go through the components of a deal and see how they can add up to the kind of offer you will be satisfied with on your book:

1. Your advance. The practice of paying an advance against anticipated royalties from a book started in the 1870s. Ever since, books have earned income to recoup the advance in two basic ways: royalties from sales of copies of the publisher's edition of the book, and income from the publisher's licensing of rights to your book that you permit your publisher to retain.

What will determine the size of the advance for your book? A combination of factors, including—

> how many copies the book is expected to sell in its first printing or its first year's sales, minus a reserve against returns of unsold books from booksellers;

its backlist potential: how long it will sell in stores, schools, or other markets;

in a hard-cover deal, its subsidiary-rights potential, principally book-club and mass-market paperback sales, and perhaps foreign-rights sales.

These key evaluations are themselves reached through other decisions:

How strong your proposal or manuscript is from a literary and/or commercial point of view

The enthusiasm the book generates in the editor and the rest of the house

How ripe the time will be for the book when it is published

What groups of consumers your book appeals to and how big those groups are

How many competitive books there will be when pub date rolls around, and how much of the market they will leave for your book

How much of a readership you have created through your past work or exposure in the media

How promotable you are

What you can and will do to promote your book (promoting fiction by unknown writers is difficult)

How much promotional effort the book will require

How much editorial or production work it will need

The size of the house: the bigger the house, the larger its budget for new books tends to be; small houses, university presses, and specialized publishers are often only able to offer small advances or perhaps no advance at all.

How much money the house has at the time to invest in books. For instance, the house may have just spent a bundle on a book, or it may be the end of the year, when some houses' budgets for acquiring books are depleted.

Whether it's a hard/soft deal. In a traditional deal, a hard-cover house keeps the right to license mass-market editions of its books and split the income with authors. In a hard/soft deal, the publisher buys hard-cover and mass-market paperback rights at the same time, with the intention of publishing the mass-market edition itself.

(As I mentioned in the last chapter, this means that you receive all of the royalties on the paperback edition. If a book has strong mass-market potential, a hard/soft deal affects the size of the advance, because the publisher won't be auctioning the mass-market rights to another publisher, which would, if successful, produce income for the author.)

How well your project complements the rest of the house's books, and specifically those coming out in the same month (mass market) or on the same spring or fall list (trade paperback and hard cover) on which your book will be published. This assumes that your manuscript is ready or will be soon enough for the publisher to fit the book into a slot on its publication schedule.

How much your book competes with the house's commitment of money and energy to the rest of its books

How anxious the house is to establish a new imprint, start a series of books in a new subject area, make a splash, fill a hole in the list, please an editor, or for another internal reason

All of the elements that go into deciding how strong a commitment to make to your book boil down to what may be an emotionally charged mix of instinct, the lessons of the past, optimism about the future, and a string of guesstimates that more often than not turn out to be a triumph of hope over experience.

New writers often say to us: "Well, since it's my first book, I guess I won't get much money for it, will I?" Probably not, since most advances for first books are less than $10,000, but the reason is not because they're first books.

A publisher will gamble whatever they think your book is worth, regardless of whether it's your first or your fourteenth. Your agent is in a better position than you are to judge what your book is worth, to know which publishers will pay top dollar for it, to know how to persuade one of them to throw caution to the winds and take the plunge, to gauge the intensity of an editor's interest, and to push as hard as possible without blowing the deal. They also know that the size of the advance for one book may affect the next advance.

Most trade book advances are in the $2,500-$15,000 range, with the average advance from a large house around $7,500, but the advance for a literary first novel may be as little as a third of that. (In the early forties, the average advance was $500.) Advances for children's books average $1,500 to $2,500.

Keep in mind that after you have your advance, you will not receive any more money from your publisher until your book has earned the advance back either through sales of copies or through licensing of rights.

If you and your agent agree about your book's literary and commercial potential, you will avoid a sudden jolt when your agent calls with an offer. For example, if you've written your first novel and you believe it's a blockbuster, you'll be expecting six-figure offers for it. But if your agent thinks it's only another promising first novel, you'll be shocked when you get a $3,000 offer.

Your book could be worth a whole lot more or less than you imagine, but it's essential to start out heading in the same direction. Hammering out the deal for your book is the time when you, your agent, and your editor must agree on your book's probable earning potential, rather than what it will earn if it's wildly successful. To help minimize their risk, publishers tend to be conservative when estimating first printings and advances.

Once your editor accepts your manuscript, you don't have to return your advance regardless of how your book fares in the marketplace. But if there are no subsidiary-rights sales and the book fares poorly, the advance is probably the only money you will receive from the publisher. The bigger your advance, the more copies your book will have to sell and the larger the sub-rights sales will have to be for the book to earn it out.

2. *How your advance will be paid.* If your book is finished and your advance is small, you may be able to get the whole advance on signing of the contract. But advances are usually divided into two or more parts, following one of these schedules:

- Half on signing and half on acceptance of the completed manuscript
- Half on signing, a quarter on acceptance of half the manuscript, and the last quarter on acceptance of the whole manuscript
- A third on signing, a third on acceptance of half of the manuscript, and the final third on acceptance of the complete manuscript.

Sometimes a publisher will insist on waiting until publication to pay the last part of the advance.

The bigger the advance, the more likely it is that it will be divided into several parts that are spread out over a longer period of time, with parts paid on signing, on acceptance of one or more portions of the manuscript, on publication, six months after publication, or beyond that. In Simon & Schuster's $2,000,000 deal for *Contact*, Carl Sagan's first novel, the advance was spread out evenly over ten years.

When it is necessary to reduce a writer's tax burden, an agent will arrange for a writer's income to be partially deferred.

If your advance will finance the writing of your book, plan your time and figure your expenses carefully before your agent starts selling the project, so you don't get caught short and so that you and your agent know the bottom-line figure you need to complete the book.

3. *The royalties.* Your royalties will vary according to the format of your book, the discount at which it is being sold, and how and where it is sold.

Trade royalties are usually based on list or cover price of your book, so if your book costs $20 and you're earning a royalty of 10 percent per copy, your royalty is $2.

Specialized publishers and some trade publishers base royalties on the net price of a book, the discounted price they receive for the book. If booksellers buy your $20 book at the standard discount of 40 percent, they pay $12; and if your royalty rate is 10 percent of your publisher's net receipts, your royalty is $1.20.

Your agent will try to make sure that if your royalties are based on the net price of your book, the royalty scale will be the equivalent of royalties based on the list price. In our experience, however, publishers who offer net royalties pay smaller royalties.

Hard-cover royalties. Although around the turn of the century, hard-cover royalties ran as high as 25 percent, they are now usually 10 percent of the list price on the first 5,000 copies sold, 12½ percent on the next 5,000 copies, and 15 percent thereafter.

Successful authors command a straight 15 percent royalty or escalating royalties that in rare cases go even higher.

On the other hand, heavily illustrated books in any format have reduced royalties because of increased production costs. In hard cover, royalties may start at 7½ percent. Or instead of escalating to 12½ percent after the first 5,000 copies, the "break," or point at which your royalty rises, may come at 7,500 copies or more.

Do you know how a publisher test-markets a new book or author? The same way every other purveyor of products and services does: by trying it out on consumers. Unless your publisher is certain of your book's reception, the first printing of your book is a break-even trial run that enables your publisher to see if it will sell. The first printing for most hard covers will be fewer than 10,000 copies. If it sells out, you and your publisher will start making money with the second printing.

Trade-paperback royalties. The average first printing for a trade paperback is less than 20,000 copies. Royalties vary from publisher to publisher, but range from 5 to 10 percent of the list price. A typical royalty scale may start at 6 percent and rise 1 or 1½ percent after 10,000, up to 20,000 copies. It may escalate again after another 10,000 copies. A straight 7½ percent royalty is generally a preferable alternative. Unless they expect to sell tens of thousands of copies, publishers are usually reluctant to give a 10 percent royalty on trade paperbacks.

Mass-market royalties. Royalties on rack-size books also vary, running from 4 percent to as high as 22 percent of the cover price for a blockbuster. A royalty of 6 percent on the first 100,000 to 150,000 copies, and 8 percent thereafter, is typical. On books by established authors, agents aim for 10 percent thereafter. The bigger the book, the higher the royalty your agent can demand.

First printings for mass-market originals, as opposed to lead originals and major hard-cover reprints, average between 50,000 and 100,000 copies.

All these royalties are reduced for mail-order sales, for copies sold outside of the United States, and for copies sold at high discounts. Discounting is a growing problem, because publishers give high discounts to the chain stores, which may handle half of all the copies sold on a book. This means lower royalties for authors.

Depending on how much clout an agent has, the agent will try to minimize the impact of reduced royalties by asking that they never fall below less than half of your basic royalty; that they only be applied to orders of your book rather than a mixed package of your publisher's books; and that they only apply to large "single-title-only" orders outside of ordinary trade channels so that bookstore chains won't qualify for them.

4. In a hard-cover contract. How paperback income will be split.

When a hard-cover house sells the paperback reprint rights, the usual split with the author is 50-50. With sufficient leverage, this can be pushed up in steps to a 70-30 split in your favor.

John Irving's agent Peter Matson obtained the ultimate paperback split. He sold William Morrow just the hard-cover rights to *The Cider House Rules* for $1.3 million, leaving him free to sell the paperback rights separately to Bantam for another $1.3 million.

If circumstances warrant, your agent will request approval of the paperback sale for your book. When a request for approval is denied, it is usually possible to obtain the less powerful but nonetheless useful right of "consultation."

5. Rights being withheld for you. The growing importance of subsidiary rights income to publishers has elevated the status of the subsidiary rights director and increased the determination of publishers to hold onto whatever rights they can.

Your book will have primary and secondary subsidiary rights. Your publisher will expect to control the right to sell primary subsidiary rights to:

> book clubs
> clubs or periodicals that publish books in condensed form
> authors and publishers who want to use part of your book in an anthology
> paperback houses if your book is a hard cover, or hard-cover publishers if you're selling to a paperback house
> magazine and newspapers that will excerpt your book after publication; this is called second-serial rights
> companies that may reproduce part or all of the book without changing it, in all media, including records, films, audio cassettes, microfilm, and various electronic means of information

storage and retrieval. Usually, the only deviation from a 50-50 split on these rights is, as described earlier, on the paperback sale.

Depending on the situation, a publisher may ask for any or all of the secondary and possibly more profitable subsidiary rights but will normally expect an agent to keep them:

First-serial rights. This enables your agent to sell excerpts from the book to appear before publication. Except for big books, first-serial excerpts are more valuable as publicity than as a means to swell your bank account. So unless an author has strong media contacts, agents, especially those outside of New York, may elect to let publishers handle first-serial rights on an 85-15 or 90-10 split, and try to obtain an immediate pay-out on the sales, instead of having the author's share of the income go toward repaying the advance.

Foreign rights. This allows your agent's network of coagents abroad to sell your book. If your book is heavily illustrated, your publisher may feel that its investment in producing the project and its ability to arrange for foreign coeditions at Frankfurt justify their keeping foreign rights. They may be right. If your publisher does keep foreign rights, your agent will try to get you an 80-20 or even a 90-10 split instead of the 50-50 or 75-25 in the boilerplate.

Dramatic rights in all media: radio, television, film, and theater.

Merchandising rights, also called commercial exploitation, including products such as T-shirts, coffee mugs, calendars, and towels. These rights are usually valuable only after a best-selling book has created a market for items containing words or images from or based on the book.

If a publisher has proven itself effective in handling these rights, you may be better off if the publisher keeps them. If so, your agent will try for as close to a 90-10 split as possible.

Rights to new media such as software, databases, audio cassettes, and video cassettes. Video cassettes have been called "the new publishing." They don't just reproduce the text of a book, but present Jane Fonda exercising or Julia Child giving cooking lessons. Until the dust settles about the value of new rights, they can cause a tug-of-war over who gets to keep them. But agents try to stand firm about retaining rights involving more than just reproducing the text.

Your agent will withhold for you all rights not granted to the publisher. The good news is that the subsidiary rights your agent retains for you may be worth a great deal more than the rights you grant to your publisher. The bad news is that they may not become valuable until your work becomes popular or the interest in the subject of your book revives for some unexpected reason, perhaps decades from now. Your agent will stay alert to possibilities for exploiting all rights to your book.

6. *Issues particular to your book.* This includes any concerns you or your agent may have about your editor, your publisher, or how your book will be published.

If an author has been burned by a publisher who didn't promote a previous book, getting a written commitment to promotion, even if it's not a big one, may be a "deal point" or "deal breaker" with the author.

Another situation involving promotion may arise if an author has a promotable book, has done successful national publicity tours, and is anxious to tour for the new book. The author may be justified in insisting that the publisher be committed to make use of the author's experience with publicity.

One of our authors, a military historian, interviewed 150 veterans for a book and promised each of them a copy. Since the book was going to retail for more than $20, this would create a financial burden for him. We arranged for him to buy 150 "courtesy copies" at cost.

If you are signing with a publisher because of an outstanding editor, your agent will try to insert a clause in the contract giving you the right to go with the editor if the editor switches houses before your book goes into production.

The issues contracts can address are as varied as the writers, editors, and publishers who sign them.

Reaching for the Stars

Obtaining the following concessions requires extra leverage:

7. *Expense money.* Your agent may be able to get you additional money to cover part or all of your out-of-pocket expenses such as travel, illustrations, and permissions costs. Although you should start out assuming that you will have to pay for expenses out of your advance, your agent will try to wrangle at least some expense money out of the publisher. It may be accounted for as an additional recoupable part of your advance, but if a publisher wants your book badly enough, the tab may be picked up for part or even all of your expenses, and folded into the overall cost of the book. The trade-off: This raises the price of the book, which in turn may affect sales.

8. *Advance escalators for appearances on the best-seller list.* This escalator and the next one usually only come into play with potential best sellers and best-selling authors who are in a position to insist on them. They are also occasionally useful for bridging the gap of expectations between an author and a publisher who is offering an advance lower than the author wants. Publishers don't mind agents reaching for the stars and making authors feel good by granting impressive escalators, because they only have to pay off if the sales happen, and then they won't mind spreading the wealth.

The numbers vary from publisher to publisher and book to book, but the basic notion is: When your book appears on *The New York Times* best-seller list, the publisher increases your advance depending on your book's position and longevity on the list. Best-seller escalators generally run from $2,500 to $10,000 a week. For a book that's number-one on the list, this could jump as high as $50,000 a week. These escalators usually have a ceiling, and the number of weeks your publisher will pay these additional advances is also open to negotiation.

9. An advance escalator on a movie sale. A movie escalator is a fixed sum, perhaps $25,000, paid when a movie based on your book goes into production. Note that neither selling the book as a film, casting the movie, nor completing the script warrants payment of the escalator, because the movie still may not be made. It's only when shooting begins that a publisher can be reasonably certain that, even if the film fails, it will at least be made. Because publishers don't like gambling with movie escalators, payment is sometimes keyed to the release of the film.

10. A promotion budget for the book. A publisher won't usually commit itself in the contract to an advertising campaign or publicity tour unless a major project or author is involved, it's an essential or deal point for the author, or the book or author presents an obvious promotion opportunity for the publisher. If an author is a celebrity or has guaranteed promotion potential, the publisher may insist that the author make a commitment to promoting the book. The publisher of a diet book even insisted on a clause that committed the author to a weight limit while she was promoting the book.

Top authors may coast to the best-seller list with $100,000 promotion campaigns you can see advertised in *Publishers Weekly*. But even if editors won't put a promotion budget in the contract, they will certainly discuss the publisher's plans for the book if they have any, and may be willing to state them in a letter, which will carry moral if not legal weight when the time comes.

11. A first printing. Again, only big books need apply for a contractual commitment to a first printing, and if a book is big enough, the commitment isn't necessary. But large publishers do base their advances partly on the royalties generated in the first year or by the first printing. Editors estimate the printing and the other deal points in a proposal-to-publish form they have to fill out to persuade the editorial board to buy a book. Your agent will ask about the estimated first printing and cover price to see if your advance is in line with your anticipated royalties. But printing estimates are as definite as next April's weather, until just before the presses roll.

Unless a publisher is committed to force-feeding books into the stores, the first printing of your book will equal the advance sale, or "laydown"—the number of books the sales reps have gotten into the stores—plus enough additional copies to cover expected reorders.

Translating from Legalese into Dollars

After going over the deal with your editor, your agent will explain it to you and discuss what changes might be possible. Usually editors don't have a great deal of latitude in upping an offer, but your agent will try for whatever improvements you agree are worth a shot.

Even when the terms of the deal are settled to the satisfaction of you and your agent, the negotiations are usually not finished. If your agent has already dealt with your publisher before, it may be possible to use a previous contract as a model and just fill in the information pertaining to the new book. Your agent will check the last contract a client signed with the publisher and negotiate necessary changes.

When it's not possible to use a previous contract as a model, after the foregoing points have been agreed on, the editor sends your agent the filled-in contract so that he or she can review the rest of the clauses.

This leads to at least one long phone conversation, perhaps preceded by a letter listing the changes your agent wants. Additional phone calls and letters may be required. Sometimes someone in the publisher's contracts department goes over the offending clauses with your agent, and they thrash out a contract both of you can live with.

Some computer publishers use computers to insert changes in their contracts, so every contract looks made-to-order. But most publishers have their contracts printed, so they look as if they were carved in stone.

Other Major Contract Clauses

Contracts are written to favor publishers, so publishers expect agents to try to negotiate a contract as favorable to their authors as they can. Your contract may contain anywhere from ten to more than a hundred clauses. The following section will explain the significance of the most important clauses and indicate the improvements your agent will bargain for.

The Grant of Rights

The book contract you sign gives your publisher the right to edit, produce, sell, and promote your book and license subsidiary rights.

Your publisher will expect to keep the right to sell its own and its licensees' editions of your book exclusively in the United States, its possessions, Canada, and the Philippines, and nonexclusively throughout the rest of the world.

Your agent will try to divide the book's subsidiary rights as described earlier.

Copyright

Unless you are writing a book for a flat fee, either because you are ghosting it for someone who can't write or because it's a work-for-hire project done on assignment or as part of your job, the copyright for your books should always be in your name. Copyright protects your ownership of and financial interest in the material. Your publisher will insert a copyright notice in your book when it is published.

Delivery of the Manuscript

Your contract will call for a manuscript of a specified length to be delivered by a specified date, on which you, your agent, and your editor agree. The contract will call for it to be delivered "in form and content satisfactory to the Publisher," or words to that effect.

This clause is a potential can of worms, because it enables an editor to reject your manuscript for reasons that have nothing to do with the manuscript: the appearance of competitive books, the publisher having changed hands or changed direction, or the condition of the book business or of the publisher's finances.

If your manuscript is rejected, your agent will serve as a second reader who can be objective about its merits and object strenuously if it is not rejected for a valid reason. The problem of acceptance is an important example of a situation in which an agent's experience, creativity, relationship with an editor, and clout with a publisher may yield a solution that will save your book.

Your publisher is justified in asking for your advance back if you don't deliver the manuscript. Unless getting a book out by a certain time is essential to its success, publishers usually accept books being late. If your book is going to be late, decide on a new completion date with your agent and editor, and get a written confirmation of the new deadline in case a question arises about it later.

Editors like predictability in their lives. If you know you will be late, give your editor as much advance warning as possible. This makes it easier to reschedule your book with a minimum of strain.

Your agent will try to commit your publisher to responding to your manuscript within a specific time period. If you're like most writers, nothing is more agonizing than waiting to hear what an editor thinks of your book. Another problem arises if your editor feels that your manuscript doesn't deliver what you promised. You are entitled to editorial feedback on your manuscript, most likely in the form of a written critique, and the opportunity to improve it. The problem remains, however, if your attempt to revise it according to the editor's directions still fails to convince the editor that it's publishable.

This problem can be avoided. If you are revising a complete manuscript, make sure that you, your agent, and your editor share an editorial vision of what you want your book to be, that the editor's written instructions accurately reflect this vision, and that your revision lives up to what your editor is expecting from you. If you are writing from a proposal, turn in what your proposal promises. If you come up with a better approach to your book, get your editor to agree in writing to your new plan for the book.

Although your publisher has a right to be satisfied with the manuscript for which it's paying, your agent will try to make sure that you have the right to approve the final copy-edited text of your book. Some contracts give you this right. It is, after all, your book, not the publisher's, and you are entitled to the final word.

Your agent will also request that your advance, or only part of it, be repayable out of the proceeds from the resale of an unsatisfactory manuscript. If your agent sells the book to another publisher, the first publisher gets its money back. No resale, no repayment. Some publishers won't agree to this arrangement unless the writer has a track record.

I try to believe that no matter what happens, it's somehow all for the best. (This is much easier to do when you're contemplating someone else's misfortune rather than your own.) But reselling an unwanted manuscript to an editor who is eager for it will assure a better fate for you and your book. If your agent can't resell the book, perhaps you or your agent can figure out a way to salvage the idea, the structure, or part of the book and resell it in article form or as another book.

Title and Cover Approval

Your agent will get you the right of consultation on, if not approval of, the title and cover of your book. Titles and covers can cause headaches for everyone. Everyone involved with your book wants it to have the strongest possible title and cover. The problem occurs when you and your publisher don't agree on what that means.

The sales department often has the last word, because if the sales manager says that the reps won't be able to get a book into the stores with a certain title or cover, it usually doesn't have a prayer. Here is another opportunity for your agent to serve as a knowledgeable, creative, objective buffer between you and the house.

Revised Editions

To prevent your book from becoming unsalable because it's outdated, the contract may commit you either to revise your book or take reduced royalties if you are unwilling or unable to revise it and your publisher has the work done by a third party. Your agent will ask that you and your publisher agree on the need for a revision and that the revision be arranged on mutually agreeable terms.

Legalities

May your life be filled with lawyers. —A Mexican curse

People joke that you can't really say you've made it until you've been sued. This criterion would make major New York houses unqualified successes, because they are sued constantly. Typically, it's the author whom plaintiffs are angry at, but the publisher always get sued too. Why? When the notorious Willie Sutton was asked why he robbed banks, he replied: "Because that's where the money is."

Few books cause legal action, and most suits publishers are hit with are nuisance suits (that's what lawyers wear to argue a small case) without merit that are settled out of court. And although publishers have insurance to help them, they still spend thousands of dollars a year fending off absurd claims. Worse yet, as the country's law schools continue to issue J.D.'s (that's a degree, not an epithet), America is becoming an increasingly litigious country. So publishers are justifiably concerned about a book's potential to cause legal action.

To limit its liability, every publisher has a warranty and indemnity clause, which basically contains the following assurances:

- You warrant that the book is yours and that you will get permission to use copyrighted material (material owned by others).
- You warrant that your book contains nothing obscene or libelous, and that it won't invade anyone's privacy.
- You agree to indemnify your publisher—that is, pay for all legal judgments, settlements, and other expenses, mainly attorney's fees—if you have breached your warranty.

Some agreements require you to pay simply because a third party says you have breached a warranty, whether or not you have actually done so. Therefore, with respect to court judgments against your publisher, your agent will ask to insert the words "finally sustained judgments" into the clause if they're not in the boilerplate, and will try to limit your liability to all or part of the income earned through the contract. The phrase "finally sustained" means that the highest court appealed to sides with the plaintiff. Fortunately, this rarely happens, because few cases get that far. Most are settled before trial.

Your agent will also try to get you the right to approve any settlement that will cost you money. Often, if you're unwilling to accept a settlement your publisher thinks is fair, you will have to post a bond to cover the potential loss if you have guessed wrong about the suit's outcome.

The most favorable outcome to your agent's negotiations with your publisher on this clause will *likely* be the following:

1. If a judgment is finally sustained or the case is settled with your approval, you pick up the entire tab.
2. Any other outcome and the cost, including expenses, is evenly divided between you and your publisher.

It costs $15,000-20,000 just to get a case to court, and although controversy can sell books, a lawsuit can destroy its momentum, leaving the book and your royalties on hold, perhaps until the suit is resolved. A positive trend: Publishers insure themselves against suits, and a growing number of them are adding authors to their liability coverage.

What can you do to prevent legal problems? Two things:

1. If you think your book may cause legal problems, find an experienced literary attorney to go over your proposal or manuscript and follow his or her recommendations for changes. When you submit your project, mention that your lawyer has reviewed it.

2. If libel is your concern, and your publisher's insurance won't cover you, do what publishers do—get libel insurance.

The Option

Like your agent, your publisher invests time and money in you and your book in the hope of creating a long relationship. If you are pleased with what your publisher has done for you and your book, you have a moral, if not legal, obligation to offer your publisher your next book.

If the publisher doesn't do right by you, you shouldn't have to be forced to have that house publish your next book. Agents try to delete the option clause unless a publisher is making a large enough investment in your book to justify at least allowing a look at your next one.

But even if an option clause remains in your contract, your agent will try to limit it to cover only similar books, and to a thirty- to sixty-day period in which to arrive at mutually agreeable terms.

The reality of the option clause is that even if it's in your contract, if you have a legitimate reason for not wanting your publisher to do your next book, a responsible publisher will not hold you prisoner.

Accounting

Your publisher will send you a royalty statement twice a year. Although it varies, most large publishers account for January-to-June sales in October and for July-to-December sales in April. The accounting covers sales of the book itself and subsidiary-rights sales.

If your book has earned back its advance and kept selling, you will also receive a check. Royalty statements have never been as clear or complete as they should be, and computers haven't helped much.

Publishers continue to draw interest every day that money sits in their banks rather than yours, so some houses hang on to it as long as possible. Someone once told me about a major publisher who only hires inexperienced accountants, so he can break them in right and teach them the house's shady approach to royalties. One of his lessons: Don't send a check until you get the third call.

Some publishers' statements are intentionally faulty, but any publisher can make a mistake. Your agent will, and you should, check your royalty statements carefully. Two signs of an honest publisher are the willingness to answer questions and rectify mistakes promptly.

Your agent will make sure that the contract contains a clause giving an accountant you choose the right to inspect your publisher's books. The clause should also state that the publisher will pay for the accounting if your royalty statement is more than 5 percent off the mark. Unfortunately, since an audit of a publisher's books may cost several thousand dollars, an audit only makes sense if large royalties are involved.

The Agent's Clause

This states that your agent represents you, and can speak, act, and receive mail and money, acting as agent on your behalf. Those agents without separate written agency agreements with their clients may also use this clause to spell out their commission arrangements. An example of this is the clause in Appendix A.

Reversion of Rights

If your publisher's edition is out of print and your book is not available in any licensed edition, this clause enables your agent to get your rights back on the book, although the process is often cumbersome and time-consuming. This clause also enables you to buy remaining copies and the production material if your agent wants to try to sell the book to another publisher.

Through experience and by sharing information with colleagues, agents develop tricks of the trade, making changes in existing clauses or adding special clauses or "riders" they have requested. Here are two examples: a clause requiring your publisher to obtain your approval to sell advertising in your book, and a "pass-through" clause, enabling you, usually once your advance has been earned back, to receive your subsidiary-rights income when your publisher receives it, instead of waiting for your next royalty statement.

This overview of contracts has only scratched the surface, but it should prove that the contract you sign may be far different from the one your agent receives. For more on the subject, I recommend another book in the Writer's Basic Bookshelf series: Richard Balkin's *How to Understand and Negotiate a Book Contract or Magazine Agreement.*

Reading Between the Lines

A publisher's contract may have ironclad clauses that will either take too long to change or that the publisher would rather lose a book over than tamper with. But most clauses in a contract can be changed if your agent has enough leverage, knowledge, skill, and creativity. The more your publisher wants your book, the more willing it will be to modify its contract in your favor. Houses vary in how flexible they are about changing their contracts, and contracts themselves evolve as publishers respond to changes in the health of the book business, the outcome of litigation, and the creation of new rights.

A sentence in a book may be all that's needed to change a contract. A cookbook from a major publisher inadvertently instructed its readers to allow a crock pot to blow its top. This led to a recall of the cookbook and a clause in contracts absolving publishers from legal responsibility for injuries caused by mistaken directions in their books.

Until it is interpreted by a court, a contract is only as binding as the good faith of the people who sign it. If you or your publisher want to find a way to cheat each other, you will.

Your agent's goal is to get you the best possible deal. But the aim of negotiating a contract is not to nail your publisher to the wall. That would be winning a battle but losing the war. Except for those terms you and your agent regard as essential to the deal, a spirit of compromise should pervade the negotiations. Your agent's success at obtaining changes requested in your contract will depend on how realistic they are and how badly the publisher wants your book.

At the end of the negotiations, you, your agent, and your publisher must remain enthusiastic about the sale and one another. Your agent helps here, as throughout the publishing process, by serving as a buffer, a lightning rod to absorb problems that arise in working out a satisfactory contract.

You and your editor would find it hard to discuss your manuscript if you've just had a knock-down drag-out fight about your contract. By knowing how much give-and-take there is in contract negotiations in general and in your publisher's contract in particular, your agent helps you begin your relationship with your publisher in a positive frame of mind, ready to tackle the challenge of making your book successful in a crowded, competitive marketplace. That's the real feat!

I hope this chapter has given you the perspective on contracts you need to understand how an agent goes about negotiating a deal. The process can take minutes or months, depending on the size of the deal and the publisher. But when your agent, your publisher, and, most important to all, you are happy with the results, congratulations are in order. You may have turned a minefield into a gold mine.

CHAPTER ELEVEN

Goals to Go: Know Yourself

When someone asked the Hungarian author Ferenc Molnar how you become a writer, he replied: "The same way you become a prostitute. First you do it for the love of it. Then you do it for a few friends and finally you do it for money."

Who is the most important person in the publishing process? You are! And you must never forget that.

If you don't believe me, read the words of Walter Meade, Hearst executive and former president of Avon Books:

> The future in publishing belongs to the same people to whom its past belongs: writers. The heart of publishing, its substance, is still the word, the sentence, the paragraph, the artful manipulation of narrative that produces entertainment or enlightment and sometimes both. . . . A house which takes pains to cultivate new and unknown writers is doing the arduous work of dedicating itself to future readers. . . . The eighties will be an exciting and exacting time for publishers; it will be a decade of unimagined opportunity for writers.

Taking Inventory

Life, like art, should be the celebration of a vision. If you're ready to take advantage of the writing opportunities waiting for you, you should have a vision of yourself and your goals as a person and a writer. To be a successful writer, you must know who you are and what you want.

Writing the lists that follow will enable you take an inventory of yourself and your goals. Take the time to write your responses to these questions and checklists. What you know about yourself is far more important than what you know about agenting, writing, and publishing.

Mozart said: "When I am . . . completely myself my ideas flow best and most abundantly." Well, on the literary chorus line of life, who are you, anyway? Make lists of your strengths and weaknesses as a person and a writer. What are the strengths you need to be a writer? A knowledge of books, writing, and what you're writing about, perhaps a desire to teach. In what areas do you feel you need improvement? Make lists of your personal and professional frailties and strong points.

The NIDY Gritty School of Writing

The NIDY (noninstitutional do-it-yourself) Gritty School of Writing offers the following checklist for prospective writers:

1. Something to say
2. The compulsive need to say it
3. Talent: the gift for turning ideas into words, characters, and situations, and knowing when they are right
4. Discipline
5. Persistence
6. Faith in your work
7. Trust in your instincts
8. Patience with your talent and others' appreciation of it
9. Reading
10. *The Elements of Style*, by William Strunk, Jr., and E. B. White.
11. The need to grow as a writer and the experience with art and life to do so.

Also make lists of the joys and hazards of writing. What are the hazards? Lack of feedback, no money, loneliness, typing, rewriting, smoking, coffee, alcohol, lack of confidence, getting the first sentence down, wanting to be a writer and not getting support, forcing oneself to write, hemorrhoids, backaches, eyes strain, rejection, being stuck at a desk. Can you add to the list?

What are the joys of writing? Acceptance, recognition, money, fame, freedom, independence, the chance for creative self-expression, the sense of accomplishment, the fun of research, giving birth to an idea, self-exploration, the opportunity to change lives, giving meaning to life, meeting interesting people, seeing one's name in print, and reading, buying, giving, and talking about books. What else excites you about being a writer?

(Someone is going to write a book about the joys and hazards of different jobs for people deciding what line of work to take up.)

The lists you make of your strengths and weaknesses as a person and writer and the joys and hazards of writing will help convince you that you have what it takes to make the grade. They must also justify your efforts. Keep these lists handy. Refer to them and revise them as needed.

Om on the Keys

In Alan Lakein's book, *How to Get Control of Your Time and Your Life,* he recommends that you ask yourself three questions:

1. What are your lifetime goals?
2. How would you like to spend the next five years?
3. How would you like to live if you knew you would be dead six months from today?

From the answers to these three questions, which he advises you ask yourself daily, you develop a daily priority list of A's, B's, and C's. You do the A's first, the B's next, and if you hold off on the C's long enough, they either become B's or they go away.

Keeping in mind the need to harmonize the short view and the long view, make lists of your immediate and long-term personal goals. Does writing fit into them well? As for your literary goals, author Shirley Fader once noted that every writer marches to a slightly different drummer.

There's a William Hamilton cartoon in which a young writer is musing wistfully to a companion: "Fame is such a hollow goal. 'Cult figure' may be enough."

Evelyn Waugh once confessed that "I was driven into writing because I found it was the only way a lazy and ill-educated man could make a decent living."

William Faulkner felt: "Really the writer doesn't want success. . . . he knows he has a short span of life, that the day will come when he must pass through the wall of oblivion, and he wants to leave a scratch on that wall—Kilroy was here—that somebody a hundred, or a thousand years later will see."

What is the beat of your drummer? You can sum up your literary goals and your means to achieving them with the answers to the following eight questions. Start each answer with the word *I* and be specific. Answering these questions is an essential step in becoming a successful writer. Your agent may ask you these questions, and you won't come across as a professional unless you have ready answers. The answers will also help clarify what you want your agent to accomplish for you.

1. Why do you want to write?

You've already listed the joys of writing. Why do you want to be a writer?

2. What literary forms—poetry, novels, nonfiction, plays, screenplays—do you want to write in?

The easiest question.

3. What do you want your writing to communicate?

Knowledge, your philosophy, the variety and inexhaustible richness of people and life?

4. What do you want your writing to achieve?

Herman Melville once wrote: ". . . it is my earnest desire to write those sort of books which are said to 'fail.' " His desire was granted with *Moby Dick*, which failed when it was published in 1851. Melville died forty years later without the recognition he deserved.

Do you want your writing to provide pleasure, bring about social change, help people enjoy better lives?

5. Who are you writing for?

An editor once told writer Arky Gonzales: "The subtle difference between a writer and an amateur is that amateurs feel and write for themselves; professional writers write for somebody else. This difference comes across in the very first or second line of an outline or manuscript."

Are you writing to be read or are you writing to fill your desk drawer? Your audience will determine what you write and how you write it.

6. How much money a year do you want to earn from your writing?

The shortest answer of the eight. Whether you want to earn a hundred or a million dollars a year, pick a number. Your agent may be able to give you a more realistic outlook. If, for instance, you want to earn $100,000 a year writing poetry, you'd better go back to the drawing board.

7. Do you want to self-publish, package your book, pay to be published, or be paid to be published?

In *Megatrends*, John Naisbitt says that we're evolving from an either/ or society to one with multiple options. This is already a reality when it comes to getting your books published.

You can self-publish them, which, thanks to the growth of personal computers and short-run printing, thousands of writers are doing.

You can package them; that is, do a proposal and find a publisher to finance the writing of the manuscript and its delivery in one of four forms: as a complete manuscript, as a copy-edited manuscript ready to be typeset, as a camera-ready mechanical ready to print, or as bound books.

You can pay part of the publishing costs to a subsidy publisher or all of the publishing costs to a vanity publisher.

You can have your book published by a small house, a large one, a regional publisher, a national one, a scholarly or university press, or a religious house.

You have to decide how involved you want to get with the publishing process.

8. How will you support your writing until it can support you?

Author Bill Paxson has observed: "If you want to write, it's like being a drug addict. You need money to support the habit."

A free-lancer has been called a writer with a working spouse. *Writer's Digest* once ran a cartoon in which a wide-eyed lady is sitting next to a man at a party and says: "I'm so thrilled to meet an author. What do you do for a living?"

If you must just jump into being a full-time writer, you may find yourself in the position of the guy at the bar in another *Writer's Digest* cartoon who laments to a fellow tippler: "Since I started freelancing full-time, I've made quite a few sales . . . my house, my car, my furniture . . ."

Most writers must face this question: How are you going to work to buy writing time? Unless you have an independent source of income or a patron, you have to have steady work. Then, as your writing income grows from being gravy to bringing home the meat and potatoes, you can cut back on other work and concentrate on your writing.

The answers to these questions should produce a coherent picture of your literary and financial goals. They should strike a realistic balance between writing for yourself and writing for the marketplace.

Put this list on the wall wherever it is that you write. Make it your personal set of affirmations, your literary mantra. Whenever you begin to wonder who you are or why you're writing, read the answers aloud to yourself. If the answers stop inspiring your best work, it's time to find new answers or another line of work.

You, Ink

It's been said that if writers were good business people, they'd have too much sense to be writers. But unless you're one of the lucky few who doesn't have to be concerned about making a living, it's important for you to think about business as well as writing. There's an entrepreneurial explosion going on that is part of the megatrend of America's going from an institutional to a self-help society.

Start thinking of yourself as an entrepreneur, a self-employed professional running a small business. Balance your desire to write something and the satisfaction of doing it well and seeing it published against your potential compensation and how the project will help develop your craft and your career, how it will help you reach your goals.

Do you have well-designed business cards saying you're a writer? What about stationery? Well, if you don't already have them, get thee to a printer.

As for being an entrepreneur, here is some excellent advice from Jay Levinson, author of *Earning Money Without a Job*. He advises would-be entrepreneurs to figure out three things:

1. How you want to live.
2. How much it costs to live that way.
3. How to earn that much money.

He offers two tips on being an entrepreneur. The first is to be modular. For instance, Jay writes advertising copy, but he also gets jobs producing television commercials, not because he does every part of the job himself but because he has developed a network of professionals he can call upon when needed. That's being modular.

Jay's other tip is to do not just one thing, but perhaps as many as ten, so you're not dependent on only one source of income. Jay writes advertising copy and books, lectures, has a direct-mail business, and self-publishes books, among other things.

If all you want to write is fiction, then you just have to keep writing it until you're successful. But if you write nonfiction, there are two contradictory approaches to developing your business, both of which have merit.

One is to develop a specialty. Once you've done one book on a subject, you're an authority and can present yourself as an expert when you try to sell your next book or article on the subject. After writing *Earning Money Without a Job,* Jay wrote three other books for entrepreneurs: *555 Ways to Earn Extra Money* and *Guerrilla Marketing: Secrets for Making Big Profits from Your Small Business, Quit Your Job/Making the Decision, Making the Break, Making it Work.*

As a writer, your capital is your time, your ideas, and your ability to turn your ideas into salable material. Examine your ideas with an eye to recycling them in as many media as possible: articles for American and foreign trade and consumer magazines and newspapers that can later be rewritten and resold, books, software, television, movie, video and audio cassettes. Pick the right subject, and you can carve a career out of it.

Carol Cartaino, former Editor-in-Chief at Writer's Digest Books, suggests the opposite tack: Don't get fixed on a certain subject. There are many subjects and kinds of writing that can be developed to make a living.

Whether or not you choose a specialty, after you've written one book, you can go from book to book and advance to advance. If you, your agent, or your editor has ideas and you put together a proposal, you can jump from one project into the next.

The Chains that Bind

What are the two biggest book chains in the world? I'll give you a clue: They're invisible.

They're the chains that link writer and reader in the transmission of an idea. Between writer and reader may come an agent; then all of the staff and free-lance specialists who provide services for a publisher: an editor, copy-editor, designer, production director, printer, sales reps, subsidiary-rights people, a publicist, an advertising manager; then, after the book exists: reviewers, distributors, and booksellers.

Each link in the publishing chain that comes between your idea and the communication of that idea to readers is either a barrier or a catalyst, depending on the person's competence, receptivity, and perseverance.

The publishing process creates five "power points." The first is when you write the book or the proposal for it. At this juncture, you have complete control over the project. The second arrives if you hire an agent. The agent decides which editors and houses to submit the book to and negotiates the sale, which usually seals its fate. The third power point comes as you work with an editor to develop the manuscript. With your editor's help, you determine the final shape of your book. The fourth power point occurs when your manuscript is in the hands of the publisher. Now it's the publisher's passion, skill, and creativity in producing and marketing the book that usually determines how it will be received by reviewers, booksellers, and book buyers.

The last and ultimate power point is reached when people pick up your book and read it. If they like it enough, regardless of what has happened to the book until then, they will start an invisible book chain of their own, by telling everyone they know that they must read the book. It's not writers or publishers who keep books alive; it's readers.

Aiding the transformation of ideas into books of lasting value is an abiding source of satisfaction for agents. But as a writer, you are the first and most important link to come between your idea and your readers. How well you develop your idea will determine its reception by the next link in the chain. This is where craft comes in.

CHAPTER TWELVE

Writers Do It Every Day: Develop Your Craft

To write simply is as difficult as to be good.
                                        —Somerset Maugham

I try to leave out the parts that people skip.
                                        —Elmore Leonard

Here is the best piece of advice in this book: Don't submit *anything* to an agent or editor until it's as well conceived and crafted as you can make it.

The document you submit to an agent or editor should create as much excitement as possible about the book and not give anyone who sees it a reason to turn it down.

One of the first questions agents and editors ask themselves about a manuscript as they read it is: How much work will it take to make this manuscript salable? The more work it will take, the less eager they will be to take it on.

A book basically offers one of two benefits: Nonfiction provides information; fiction, entertainment. Ultimately, a book has only two elements: an idea and the execution of that idea. Your job is to generate an idea and execute it so that your book delivers the benefit you intend as compellingly as possible. This takes *craft*.

Developing Your Craft

There are nine facets to developing your craft:

Reading. Ernest Gaines, author of *The Autobiography of Miss Jane Pittman*, pinpoints two of them in what he calls "The Six Golden Rules of Writing: Read, read, read, and write, write, write." He believes that you can only write as well as you read. Writers always have reasons to read: pleasure, information, inspiration, research.

Ray Bradbury recommends that, in addition to learning about all of the arts, writers take half an hour every night and read one poem, one essay, and one short story, both for pleasure and to stoke the fires of the imagination.

When it comes to selling your project, the bad news, as I mentioned earlier, is that your book will compete with every other book that editors and their editorial boards know about. That's thousands of books, and the number keeps growing.

The good news is that for virtually anything you want to write, models—both bombs and best sellers—abound. You can read comparable books so you can do something different and better.

You can also learn how to evaluate style and content and assimilate the criteria needed to judge how your work measures up. Become an expert on the kind of books you want to write, and you will discover that there's nothing mysterious about what makes publishable prose. What works for you in the books you admire will work for your readers.

Coming up with ideas. Reading books and news media is an inexhaustible source of ideas. One of my favorite *New Yorker* cartoons shows two women nursing cocktails and one is saying to the other: "I'm marrying Marvin. I think there's a book in it." There's a book in just about anything. In *The Craft of Writing*, William Sloane remarks: "There are no uninteresting subjects, only uninteresting writers."

Is it hard for you to find salable book ideas? If so, the following lists will help you generate ideas:

What kinds of books do you like to read? What reading experiences bring you the most pleasure? What do you most enjoy reading about?

Sex	Science
Love	Technology
Adventure	Social progress
People overcoming obstacles	The family
Mysteries	International intrigue
Self-improvement	Inspirational writing
Humorous situations	A hobby or personal interest
Spirituality	Crime
Business	Money
Politics	The wealthy
Use and abuse of power	Good triumphing over evil
Exposés	Travels to exotic settings
The arts	Biographies
History	Family sagas
The future	The rise of heroic figures

Use this list as a basis for making one of your own, and rest assured that, since you are a member of the human family, what interests you interests millions of other readers too.

Make a list of all of your favorite books, beginning with the first one you can remember, and explain why you like each book. Both of these lists are what inspire you to write, because you will enjoy writing what you like to read most, and your passion will inspire your best efforts. And your best efforts will inspire your agent's.

Willa Cather believed that most of the basic material a writer works with is acquired before the age of fifteen. J.P. Donleavy made a cynical observation along the same lines: "Writing is turning one's worst moments into money." Philip Roth summed up the value of experience to writers when he said: "Nothing bad can happen to a writer. Everything is material."

Make a list of the most important moments—good and bad—in your past. Then describe how they have shaped your life and how you might be able to shape them into characters, scenes, and ideas for books.

What subjects have you written about or already have a knowledge of that could be the basis for a book? What topics interest you enough to make you want to research a book about them?

The last list requires you to look ahead and use your imagination. Keep in mind that between writing, selling, and publishing your book, two or more years may pass. Ask yourself: What will America be like in two years? What will its quarter of a billion citizens need and want to read about?

What will its concerns and opportunities be in the areas of sex, politics, religion, business, science, technology, relationships, health, crime, money, social problems, and in your personal and professional areas of interest? For a preview, read *Megatrends*. Place yourself in the position of a publisher wondering what projects to invest in and see if your list of guesses leads to the beginning of a book.

Conscientiously and creatively done, these lists will lead you to topics worth exploring. Your agent may be willing to brainstorm with you, using these lists to come up with an idea for your next book.

Like your ability to write, your ideas are your stock in trade. Keep a notebook or cassette recorder handy so you can make a note of them whenever they hit you. Keep a file of them for future reference, and don't just limit yourself to book ideas. Sooner or later, you will also find a use for ideas for scenes, settings, characters, and bits of dialogue, for anything that comes to mind that you think is worth recording. Those minutes in the morning and at night when you're drifting between being asleep and awake can be among your most creative, so be prepared.

Never suppose you are the only writer who has hit upon your idea. In our multi-media environment, we are constantly bombarded with ideas. If one is worth following up, do so as fast as possible without diminishing the quality of your work.

A publisher will buy your idea in one of two forms: a complete manuscript or a proposal. A first novel usually has to be finished. But if you have proved that you can research and write nonfiction—by selling articles, for instance—a publisher will buy your book on the basis of a proposal consisting of an introduction about the book and you, a thorough chapter-by-chapter outline, and one or two sample chapters, depending on the nature of the book.

Researching. Ernest Hemingway believed that you should know ten times as much about a subject as you put into a book. Learning all you can about a topic enriches what you write, enhances your stature as an authority, and expands the opportunities to use your knowledge for articles, seminars, publicity, and other books.

Outlining. Unless you're a novelist who has to discover what happens as you write, create the structure for your book that best suits the material. As Strunk and White suggest in *The Elements of Style*, the more thoroughly you outline your book, the greater your chances of success in writing it. Of course, you should feel free to improve the structure if a better alternative emerges. But when you set out to construct an enduring edifice of prose, give yourself a solid foundation on which to build.

Establishing a work style. Of his writing needs, Isaac Asimov commented: "The only absolute requirement I have in order to write is that I have to be awake."

What do you need in order to write? Do you have a room where you can write undisturbed? Do you write better early in the morning? During the day? At night?

Do you use a tape recorder? A pen? A typewriter? A computer?

Kahlil Gibran once wrote: "Your daily life is your temple and your religion." Write down your daily schedule, putting the hours of the day on the left side of the page and the activities next to them. Is writing one of your daily rituals? If it is, how many hours a day do you write? Two? Three? Four? More? If it isn't, now's the time to revise your schedule.

William Faulkner once said: "I write when the spirit moves and I make sure it moves every day." Regardless of when, where, and how they do it, and whether they do it for one hour or ten, writers do it every day. I keep hoping someone will make a bumper sticker out of that line and give me a royalty on it. (That and: "Editors do it between the lines.")

Push yourself with an attainable goal for the number of pages you crank out a day and a deadline for finishing your projects. Become a dedicated word processor. Even a page a day is a book a year.

There is only one right way to write: in whatever way enables you to produce your best work. So find the time, place, and writing tools that spur your best efforts. Sticking to the work style that works for you will boost your effectiveness, morale, and professionalism.

Writing. In an article for *The Writer,* Morris West philosophized: "Writing is like making love. You have to practice to be good at it. Like the best lovemaking, it has to be done in private and with great consideration for your partner in the enterprise, who is in this case the reader."

Every line of your copy must motivate readers to keep turning the pages. An editor expects your books to be written with all the craft at your command. When, as a professional writer, you present your work to writers, agents, editors, and book buyers, your calling obliges you to offer only your best work.

Craft leaps off the page instantly. Agents and editors will be delighted if, after reading your first paragraph, they can exclaim to themselves: "At last! This one can really write!" Editors and agents who care about books are suckers for good writing.

Your style should be lucid, flowing, creative, brilliant, moving, engaging, entertaining, passionate—in a word, as irresistible as you want your reviews to be. While style is more important in a novel or a biography than in a how-to book, the more pleasurable any book is to read, the better the reviews will be and the more word-of-mouth recommendations the book will generate.

Our favorite guide to the prose of pros is *The Elements of Style.* It's a wonderful book both because its advice is sound and because it's an excellent example of what it preaches. Somerset Maugham once lamented: "There are three rules for writing the novel. Unfortunately, no one knows what they are." For a handy set of rules to write by, try this: Type the list of commandments on composition and style in *The Elements of Style* and put it up on the wall where you write. If there's something wrong with your prose, it's probably on that list.   ·

Less is more. Fine writing stands out because of its lack of faults, because authors have the taste to know when a word, sentence, or idea doesn't feel right, and the discipline to revise their work until it does.

First-time authors may find it difficult to believe, but when it comes to prose, less is more. Good writing is simple, not unnecessarily flashy; direct, not flowery; concise, with no extra words.

Writers with computers must be careful to avoid being seduced by the ease of inserting new material into a manuscript. If you're going to add something, make sure more will be better, not just bigger.

Besides brevity, writing at its best also has passion, vision, and vigor. Editor Toni Burbank once remarked about a manuscript: "There was nothing wrong with it, but there was nothing right with it either." Or as author Cyra McFadden once lamented about another failed effort: "The prose just lay there, dead on the page."

Make your writing live for agents and editors, and if you have a salable idea, your manuscript will sell. Always write as if your future depends on it; it does.

Revising. Think of writing as having two stages: writing for fact and writing for impact. First you have to get something, anything, down on paper, and then massage it until it's 100 percent.

In her *Guide to Writing Fiction*, Phyllis Whitney advises: "Remember: good books are not written; they are rewritten." Mario Puzo stated it even more simply: "The art of writing is rewriting."

If you read *The Thorn Birds*, part of the reason you enjoyed it is because Colleen McCullough rewrote her thousand-page manuscript ten times. This is not necessarily to recommend that you do the same but to convince you that revision is the only way you will produce your best work.

Let the chance to revise your work as often as necessary liberate your creativity. Let your imagination soar in early drafts, knowing that craft will assert itself later, culling wheat from chaff. Only your last revision counts, that final reckoning when you must resolve the tension between thought and feeling and make every word count.

Keep revising your work until you're certain it's as good as it can be. That's your job, and it's the most important service you can perform for your book. When that's done, it's time to start seeing if you're right.

Sharing. By the time you've finished your manuscript, you will need a respite. You may be so close to it that you can't distinguish its faults from its virtues. If you revise a passage often enough, you know it so well that you start to see what's not there. Now's the time to give yourself a break and share your manuscript with readers who can advise you on how to improve it. Five kinds of readers await your opus:

1. Friends and family, who will tell you they like it, because they like you. After all, what are friends and family for? But you deserve encouragement, so enjoy it. At the same time, however, seek out the following critics:

2. Potential readers: They may not know good writing, but they know what they like. Would they buy your book if they found it in a bookstore?

3. Literate, objective readers who can tell you what's wrong with

your manuscript as well as what's right with it. Consider joining or starting a writers' group, a round table of writers who meet once a week to critique members' work.

4. Experts who are knowledgeable about the subject of your book or the kind of novel you are writing. If you are developing a controversial thesis, find a member of the opposition to go over it for you and try to poke holes in it. You may not gain a convert, but you might avoid embarrassing yourself later.

5. Most valuable of all, a devil's advocate. Isaac Bashevis Singer once called a wastebasket a writer's best friend. Another best friend is a devil's advocate, someone who can and will combine truth and charity and spot every word, punctuation mark, sentence structure, idea, character, or incident that can be improved or removed. Devil's advocates are worth their weight in royalties.

If you can't find anyone else, use your professional network or *Literary Market Place* and hire an experienced, reputable free-lance editor to help you purge your manuscript of imperfections.

Since reactions, especially to fiction, are subjective, receiving more than one will prepare you for the varying responses your book will arouse. You may also have to sift conflicting and possibly even confusing suggestions and follow the advice that makes the most sense to you. As in all things, you must trust your instincts.

Taking your best shot. Once you've sorted out the opinions of others and feel ready to return to your manuscript with a fresh eye, go over it again and, integrating necessary changes, do a final revision. Then it's time to see if you got it right.

CHAPTER THIRTEEN

Last Writes

A good book is the purest essence of the human soul.
　　　　　　　　　　　　　　　　　—*Thomas Carlyle*

He who obtains has little. He who scatters has much.
　　　　　　　　　　　　　　　　　　　　—*Lao-Tse*

The history of literature is nothing but the performance by authors of feats which the best experience had declared could not be performed
　　　　　　　　　　　　　　　　　　　—*Arnold Bennett*

Like agents and editors, you must develop a tolerance for uncertainty, disappointment, and rejection. Rejection comes with the territory. So while your agent is trying to place your book, or even if it doesn't sell, keep writing and take the long view. Look at a rejection as the editor's loss. Agents aren't judging you, they're judging your work, and they may be wrong. Don't regard unsold work as a failure; regard it as inventory that will one day sell.

Even if your book does sell, once you type the last period on your manuscript, it's either terminal or timeless, and there's nothing you can do about it. As Philip Roth has observed, once a book is published, the world edits it. So look at the fruits of your career not as one book but as ten or twenty, and strive to make each better than the last.

You may think it's crazy, but I think obscurity is one of a writer's greatest assets. Cherish your obscurity while you still have it. Use it to write, free from the distractions of fame and fortune and the pressure of expectations created by success. Ray Bradbury once remarked: "When you start writing, you have to learn to accept rejection. Once you're successful, you have to learn to reject acceptance."

The Literary Life

Whether you buy hard-cover books or paperbacks, whether you buy them as gifts or for yourself, buy books. Support the business you want to support you. Three of the joys of the literary life are browsing in bookstores, buying books, and building a library of books you love.

Get to know your local booksellers and make allies of them. They may share your love of books and can be valuable sources of information and encouragement. One day you may be asking them for a book-signing!

Encourage all of the people you know to read. Exchange favorite books with them. At the very least, this is a slow but a certain way to build an audience for your work.

Writing as if Books Mattered

Books are more than pleasurable companions. In 1981, at the American Book Awards ceremony in Carnegie Hall, New York's Mayor and best-selling author-to-be Ed Koch said: "Books are not the foundation of civilization, they *are* civilization."

Max Perkins was a legendary editor who worked for Scribner's. In a career that spanned three decades, he edited the work of Ernest Hemingway, F. Scott Fitzgerald, and Thomas Wolfe. In *Max Perkins: Editor of Genius*, Scott Berg's inspiring biography, Perkins says: "There is nothing so important as the book can be."

The right book, fiction or nonfiction, will change the world, and a book that changes America changes the world, because America is leading the world into the future.

Norman Mailer believes that "only great fiction can save the world . . . For fiction still believes that one mind can see it whole."

The world is changing faster than ever and more than ever, readers of all ages around the world need writers with vision, reporters and storytellers, to explain what's going on and how to survive and thrive as the age of information transforms our lives.

Rarely has the planet needed calming, reassuring, inspiring voices more than now. There is an urgent need for us to understand ourselves, our neighbors, Americans everywhere, and the rest of the human family. As the planet hurtles through time and space on this voyage of transformation, Spaceship Earth has no more valuable resource than its artists and writers, who should be its copilots.

But even if you are not fated to write books that improve the human condition, writing any book well is an achievement you can be proud of. Writing is a courageous calling, and if you can add to the world's store of pleasure and information, of beauty and truth, your future is assured.

If your books are touched with the magic of capturing the people, ideas, and situations they describe in a compelling, timeless, universal way, they will endure. What greater challenge can you want? What greater achievement can you hope for?

The Age of the Writer

If you are lucky enough to be able to write, you have been endowed with a wonderful gift. You owe it to yourself and posterity to develop that gift to its fullest, to place your life in the service of your gift, your ideas, and your readers.

But don't let your writing turn you into a one-sided personality. Strive to develop all of your potentials as a human being. Your development as a writer will mirror your personal growth.

Writing is the easiest of the arts to enter and succeed in. Commiserate with an artist, actor, dancer, or composer if you don't believe it. And now is the most exciting time ever to be alive and the best time ever to be a writer. The age of information is also the age of the writer.

There are more subjects to write about, more forms and formats for your books to be published in, more agents, more publishers, and more ways to get your books published, promote them, and make money from them than ever before. And computers have ended most of the craft's mechanical drudgery.

Where authors and publisher are one is in their need to sustain a relentless, self-renewing, passionate sense of mission: to write and publish out of what is best in themselves for what is best in their readers.

Always remember that as a writer, you are the most important person in the publishing process, because you make it go. The tougher the book business gets, the more agents' and editors' jobs hinge on their ferreting out good books and new writers.

Promising new writers are the lifeblood of the publishing and agenting business. Agents and editors are as delighted to find promising new writers as new writers are to be published. Selling a well-conceived, well-written book that satisfies readers' insatiable need for understanding and entertainment is easier than ever.

An agent can speed up this process by knowing which editors and publishers to avoid and approach, so that whether it's the first editor who buys your manuscript or the twentieth, he or she will be the best possible editor at the best possible house for you and your book. An agent will also make sure that you are as fairly compensated for your efforts as possible.

Chapter 9 describes a book's six lunges at the brass ring of best sellerdom. One more lunge is essential: The strongest hope your books will have of reaching their literary and commercial potential is for you to stretch your abilities to their limits. Conceive and craft your books as well as you can. Submitting only your best work will bring out the best in every agent and editor who reads it.

Hundreds of agents and editors across the country are hungry for new writers. If you have enough talent and persistence, an agent and an editor, properly presented with the right manuscript at the right time, will take on your book. Since rejecting even best sellers is a publishing tradition, no matter how many times your work is rejected, you must keep writing and console yourself with the certainty that persistence rewards talent.

A respected editor used to offer the following advice to aspiring writers: "If anything can stop you from becoming a writer, let it. If nothing can stop you, do it and you'll make it."

I hope that you will let nothing stop you, that no matter what you write, you will commit yourself to becoming the best writer you can be, not just for yourself, but for all of us.

Appendix A: Agent's Clause

Agents who don't have written agreements with their clients may, as in the following example, spell out their compensation in the agent's clause of the publisher's contract more completely than would otherwise be necessary.

The Author hereby irrevocably appoints _____ as his sole and exclusive agent with respect to the said Work and authorizes and directs the Publisher to make all payments due or to become due to the Author hereunder to and in the name of the said agent, and to accept the receipt of the said agent as full evidence and satisfaction of such payments. As sole and exclusive agent, the said agent is authorized to negotiate for the Author throughout the World as to the disposal of all other rights in and to the said Work (including without limitation works to which any option herein shall apply). The said agent is further empowered to engage sub-agents for the sale of British Commonwealth and/or translation rights in and to the said Work (and said optioned works and to pay such sub-agents a commission of up to ten percent (10%) of the monies collected from the disposition of any such British Commonwealth and/or translation rights through such sub-agents. In consideration for services rendered, the said agent is entitled to receive or retain as its commission fifteen percent (15%) of gross monies paid to the Author hereunder and from all other rights in and to the said Work (including the said optioned works), except that such commission shall be reduced to ten percent (10%) as to those monies out of which a sub-agent's commission of five percent (5%) or more is also paid, the said ten percent (10%) to be computed after deduction of the sub-agent's commissions. The provisions of this clause shall survive the expiration of this Agreement.

Appendix B: Two Agents' Contracts

Bobbe Siegel, Rights Representative Sample Agreement

It is agreed that _____ (hereinafter referred to as the Client) does grant Mrs. Bobbe Siegel (hereinafter referred to as the Agent) the exclusive right to represent the Client in any and all negotiations for the sale of _____ (hereinafter referred to as the Work) to a publisher and, thereafter, for the sale of any and all rights related to the Work as well as all other books and/or projects as shall be mutually agreed upon.

The Client does hereby warrant that He/She is the author and sole owner of the Work; that it is original and that it contains no matter unlawful in the content nor does it violate the rights of any third party; that the rights granted hereunder are free and clear; and that the Client has full power to grant such representation to the Agent.

The Client agrees that the Agent shall receive 15% (fifteen per cent) of the gross of all monies earned from the sale of the Work. It is also agreed that the Agent will receive from the sale, licensing option or other disposition of any foreign language rights (including British rights) when negotiated without an overseas subagent a commission of 15% (fifteen per cent) of the gross; when foreign language volume rights (including British rights) are negotiated with an overseas subagent the total commission will be 20% (twenty per cent) of the gross: 10% (ten per cent) for the Agent and 10% (ten per cent) for the sub-agent. Further, if the Agent should use the services of a sub-agent for the sale of movie and/or television rights the total commission shall be 20% (twenty per cent): 10% (ten per cent) for the agent and 10% (ten per cent) for the sub-agent . . . all from the gross.

The Client does hereby empower the Agent to receive all monies due to him under any contractual arrangements related to the Work and the Agent warrants that her receipt shall be a good and valid discharge. The Client further empowers the Agent to deal with all parties on his behalf in all matters arising from the Work. The Client agrees that this agreement shall be binding on his/her estate.

The Agent agrees to remit all monies due to the Client, less the Agent's stipulated commission, within thirty (30) days of the receipt of any monies earned from the sale of any rights related to the Work if said monies are paid in U.S. currency. Otherwise, the Agent will remit all monies due to the Client, less the Agent's stipulated commission, within thirty (30) days of the conversion of said monies to U.S currency.

If either Client or Agent should desire to terminate this agreement either party must inform the other, by certified mail, of such intent, and the agreement shall be considered terminated 60 (sixty) days after receipt of such letter. It is, however, understood that any monies due after termination whether derived from contractual agreements already negotiated or under negotiation by the Agent when the agreement is terminated shall be paid to the Agent who will then deduct her commission and remit to the Client as outlined above.

If the foregoing correctly sets forth your understanding please sign both copies of this letter, where indicated, retaining one copy for your files and returning the other copy to me for mine.

Michael Larsen-Elizabeth Pomada Literary Agents: Sample Agreement

Dear Michael and Elizabeth:

While trust, friendliness, and confidence are the basis for our relationship, I have read your brochure, and I am ready to put our commitments to each other in writing.

I appoint you my sole agent to advise me and negotiate sales of all kinds for all of my literary material and its subsidiary rights in all forms and media and for all future uses throughout the world. You may appoint coagents to help you.

You have the right of first refusal on all literary material now uncommitted in which I will have any right or interest. If you decline to handle a property, I shall be free to do as I please with it without obligation to you.

If a potential buyer for my literary work or services approaches me, I will refer the buyer to you.

If an idea is mine and we do not develop it together, only I have the rights to the idea or any basic variation on it. However, if another writer approaches you with the same idea or a similar idea, you are free to represent the project. If the idea for a project is yours, only you have the rights to the idea or any basic variation on it. You may represent a project competitive to mine, provided that in your judgment, it doesn't lessen your ability to represent my work.

You will pay for all expenses which arise in selling my work except photocopying my work and mailing it abroad or on multiple submissions; buying galleys and books; and legal advice. I must approve in advance all expenses over $50 for which I will be responsible.

You may receive on my behalf all money due me from agreements signed through your efforts. This includes all sales for which negotiations begin during the term of this agreement and end within six months after it expires, and all changes and extensions in those agreements, regardless of when made, or by whom.

You are irrevocably entitled to deduct 15% commission on all gross income negotiated on my behalf, including production costs, earned through your agency.

For foreign rights, you may deduct 20%, which includes 10% for your co-agents. All commissions you receive will not be returnable for any reason.

I must first approve all offers and then sign all agreements negotiated on my behalf. Michael Larsen/Elizabeth Pomada Literary Agents will be named as my agency in all agreements I sign on all projects represented by you.

You will remit all money and statements due me within 10 working days of receiving them.

You may respond to mail received on my behalf unless it is personal, in which case you will forward it to me promptly. I will notify you promptly if I change my phone number or address.

I realize it may take years to sell a project and you agree to try as long as you believe it is possible. You will notify me promptly when you think a project is no longer salable, and then I may do with it as I wish, without obligation to you.

You or I may end this agreement with 60 days' notice by registered mail. However, you will be entitled to receive statements and commissions on all rights on properties on which you make the initial sale, whether or not the agency represents me on the sales of these rights.

This agreement is binding on our respective personal and business heirs and assigns and will be interpreted according to California law.

I am free to sign this agreement and will not agree to a conflicting obligation. I will sign two copies of this agreement and each of us will have one. Both of our signatures are needed to change this agreement.

Like you, I am signing this agreement in the hope that it will symbolize our mutual long-term commitment to the development of my career and to sharing the satisfaction and rewards of this growth.

Appendix C: Codes and Canons

Independent Literary Agents Association Code of Ethics

1. A member shall represent his or her client in a professional manner, consistent with all applicable law and in accordance with the member's fiduciary responsibility to the client. A member shall deal honorably and in good faith with other agents, publishers, and all others with whom he or she has professional dealings.

2. A member shall take responsible measures to protect the security and integrity of the client's funds. A member shall deposit funds received on behalf of the client promptly upon receipt, and shall make payments of funds due the client promptly, but in no event later than 10 business days after clearance. A member's books of account pertaining to the client shall be open to him or her at mutually convenient times.

3. A member shall inform his or her client of significant matters relating to the client's work. A member shall provide all information, including copies of agreements and royalty statements, concerning the client's work that the client shall reasonably request.

4. A member shall discuss and agree with the client at the outset of their relationship the commission and/or other compensation to be retained or received. A member shall discuss in advance those expenses that shall be paid or reimbursed by the client, which may include, among others, expenses for books and galleys, photocopies, legal fees, messenger fees, postage, long distance telephone calls, telex and cable charges.

5. A member shall not be engaged professionally, on a regular basis, not exceeding twenty percent (20%) of the member's professional activity in acquiring authors' services and rights to literary properties, as distinct from representing clients in the sale of such services or granting of such rights. The foregoing shall not apply to a member's scouting activities. A member shall disclose to his or her clients the member's professional involvement in acquiring rights to literary properties (including scouting), or engaging authors' services, at the outset of any transaction which could create a conflict of interest, or the appearance of such a conflict. Whenever a member proposes to acquire literary property from or engage the services of a client, the member shall advise the client fully of the member's role in the proposed transaction, and of the client's right to obtain separate representation therein.

Society of Authors' Representatives, Inc. *Canons of Ethics*

(as promulgated by the Committee on Ethics and Practices)

1. The members of the Society of Authors' Representatives are committed to the highest standard of conduct in the performance of their professional activities. While affirming the necessity and desirability of maintaining their full individuality and freedom of action, the members pledge themselves to loyal service to their clients' business and artistic needs, and will allow no conflicts of interest which would interfere with such service. They pledge their support to the Society itself and to the principles of honorable coexistence, directness, and honesty in their relationships with their co-members. They undertake never to mislead, deceive, dupe, defraud, or victimize their clients, other members of the Society, the general public, or any person with whom they do business as a member of the Society.

2. Members must maintain separate bank accounts so that monies due authors are not commingled with members' other funds.

3. In addition to such compensation for ordinary agency services as may be agreed upon between the individual members and their individual clients, each member may, subject to the approval of his or its client, pass along to such client charges incurred by the member on the client's behalf, such as copyright fees, manuscript retyping, machine copies, copies of books for use in the sale of other rights, long distance calls, cables, special messenger fees, and travel costs. Such charges shall only be made after first notifying the author to ensure his approval.

4. Members shall keep each client apprised of all matters entrusted to them, and shall promptly furnish such information as the author may reasonably request.

5. Members shall not represent both buyer and seller in the same transaction unless the member notifies both parties before any negotiations proceed and offers the opportunity to either party to arrange for other representation in that transaction. The member shall receive a commission or payment from only the author or the employer, not both.

6. Members may not receive a secret profit in connection with any transaction involving a client. If such profit is received, the member must promptly pay over the entire amount to the client.

7. Members must treat their clients' financial affairs as private and confidential except as required by law.

8. Payments and accounts to clients shall be rendered promptly on receipt by members within ten days unless otherwise instructed by the client. Revenues from translation rights shall be paid to the client within a reasonable time of their receipt. However, on stock and similar rights, statements of royalties and payments shall be made the month following receipt by the member, each statement and payment to cover all royalties received to the 25th day of the previous calendar month. Payments for amateur rights shall be made every six months. Members' books of accounts must be open to the client at all times with respect to transactions concerning him.

9. Where a member has a written contract with an author, it shall not be assignable by the member without the author's prior written consent, except to organizations merging with or acquiring the member, or substantially all its assets.

10. On the death of an author, the member shall continue to remit all net sums from payments made in accordance with agreements existing to the date of death.

Bibliography

Author Law and Strategies: A Legal Guide for the Working Writer, Brad Bunnin. Berkeley: Nolo Press, 1983.

The Author's Empty Purse and the Rise of the Literary Agent, James G. Hepburn. London: Oxford University Press, 1968.

The Author's Handbook, Franklynn Peterson and Judi Kesselman-Turkel. Englewood Cliffs, N.J.: Prentice-Hall, 1982.

The Bantam Story: Thirty Years of Paperback Publishing, Clarence Petersen. New York: Bantam Books, Inc., 1970.

The Beginning Writer's Answer Book, revised edition, edited by Kirk Polking, Jean Chimsky and Rose Adkins. Cincinnati, Ohio: Writer's Digest Books.

The Blockbuster Complex: Conglomerates, Show Business, and Book Publishing, Thomas Whiteside. Middletown, Conn. Wesleyan Univ. Press, 1981.

Books: From Writer to Reader, Howard Greenfield. New York: Crown Publishers, Inc., 1976.

Book Publishing: What It Is, What It Does, 2nd edition, John P. Dessauer. New York: R.R. Bowker Co., 1981.

Books: The Culture and Commerce of Publishing, Lewis A. Coser, Charles Kadushin, and Walter W. Powell. New York: Basic Books, Inc., 1982.

The Business of Being a Writer, Stephen Goldin and Kathleen Sky. New York: Harper & Row, 1982.

Chronicles of Barabbas 1884-1934, George H. Doran. New York: Harcourt, Brace and Company, Inc., 1935.

The Complete Guide to Writing Non-Fiction, The American Society of Journalists and Authors. Glen Evans ed. Cincinnati: Writer's Digest Books, 1983.

The Complete Handbook for Freelance Writers, Kay Cassill. Cincinnati: Writer's Digest Books, 1981.

Confession Writer's Handbook, Florence K. Palmer. Cincinnati: Writer's Digest Books.

Don't Step On It—It Might Be a Writer, Donald MacCampbell. Los Angeles: Sherbourne Press, Inc., 1972.

Earning Money Without a Job, Jay Conrad Levinson, New York: Holt, Rinehart & Winston, 1979.

Editors on Editing: An Inside View of What Editors Really Do, revised edition, edited by Gerald Gross. New York: Harper & Row, 1985.

The Elements of Style, 3rd edition, William Strunk, Jr., and E. B. White. New York: Macmillan Publishing Co., Inc., 1979.

Getting Published: A Guide for Businesspeople and Other Professionals, Gary S. Belkin. New York: John Wiley & Sons, 1984.

Golden Multitudes: The Story of Best Sellers in the United States, Frank Luther Mott. New York: Macmillan, 1947.

How to Become a Bestselling Author, Stanley J. Corwin. Cincinnati: Writer's Digest Books, 1984.

How to Be Your Own Literary Agent, Richard Curtis, Boston: Houghton Mifflin Co., 1983.

How to Get An Agent, Phyllis Taylor Pianka. 1985.

How to Get Control of Your Time and Your Life, Alan Lakein. New York: Signet Books, 1973.

How to Get Happily Published: A Complete and Candid Guide, Judith Appelbaum and Nancy Evans. New York: New American Library, 1982.

How to Sell What You Write, Jane Adams. New York: G.P. Putnam's Sons, 1984.

How to Understand & Negotiate a Book Contract or Magazine Agreement, Richard Balkin. Cincinnati: Writer's Digest Books, 1985.

How to Write Books that Sell: A Guide to Cashing In on the Booming Book Business, L. Perry Wilbur. Chicago: Contemporary Books Inc., 1979.

In Cold Type: Overcoming the Book Crisis, Leonard Shatzkin. Boston: Houghton Mifflin, Co., 1982.

Indecent Pleasures, William Targ. New York: Macmillan, 1975.

Inside Publishing, Bill Adler. New York: Bobbs-Merrill Company, Inc., 1982.

Law and the Writer, edited by Kirk Polking and Leonard S. Meranus. Cincinnati: Writer's Digest Books, rev. ed., 1981.

The Literary Agent and the Writer: A Professional Guide, Diane Cleaver. Boston: The Writer, Inc., 1984.

Literary Agents: A Writer's Guide, Debby Mayer. New York: Pushcart Press, 1983.

Literary Agents of North America 1984-85 Marketplace: The Complete Guide to U.S. and Canadian Literary Agencies, compiled and edited by Author Aid/ Research Associates International. New York: Author Aid/Research Associates International, 1984.

Literary Market Place: The Directory of American Book Publishing, New York: R.R. Bowker Co., 1985.

Martin Eden, Jack London. New York: Airmont Publishing Co., Inc., 1970.

Max Perkins: Editor of Genius, A. Scott Berg. New York: Pocket Books, 1978.

Megatrends: Ten New Directions Transforming Our Lives, John Naisbitt. New York: Warner Books, 1982.

The Middle Man: The Adventures of a Literary Agent, Paul R. Reynolds. New York: William Morrow, 1972.

Paperback Talk, Ray Walters. Chicago: Academy Chicago Publishers, 1985.

Publicity for Books and Authors, by Peggy Glenn. Huntington Beach: Aames-Allen Publishing Co., 1985.

Rejection, John White. Reading, Mass. Addison-Wesley, 1982.

The Rights of Authors and Artists: The Basic ACLU Guide to the Legal Rights of Authors and Artists, Kenneth P. Norwick, Jerry Simon Chasen, and Henry R. Kaufman. New York: Bantam Books, 1984.

A Talent for Luck: An Autobiography, Helen M. Strauss. New York: Random House, 1979.

This Was Publishing: A Chronicle of the Book Trade in the Gilded Age, Donald Sheehan. Bloomington: Indiana University Press, 1952.

The Truth about Publishing, Sir Stanley Unwin, London: George Allen & Unwin, Ltd., 1960.

The 29 Most Common Writing Mistakes and How to Avoid Them, Judy Delton, Cincinnati: Writer's Digest Books, 1985.

Two Bit Culture: The Paperbacking of America, Kenneth C. Davis. Boston: Houghton Mifflin Co., 1984.

What Happens in Book Publishing, Chandler Grannis. New York: Columbia University Press, 1967.

A Writer's Guide to Book Publishing, 2nd edition, Richard Balkin. New York: Hawthorn/Dutton, 1981.

The Writer's Handbook, edited by A. S. Burack. Boston: The Writer, Inc., 1977.

The Writer's Legal and Business Guide, compiled and edited by Norman Beil. A Presentation of the Beverly Hills Bar Association Barristers Committee for the Arts. New York: Arco Publishing, Inc., 1984.

The Writer's Legal Guide, Tad Crawford. New York: Hawthorn Books, Inc., 1977.

The Writer's Quotation Book: A Literary Companion, edited by James Charlton. Yonkers: The Pushcart Press, 1980, rev. ed. 1985.

The Writer's Survival Manual: The Complete Guide to Getting Your Book Published Right, Carol Meyer. New York: Crown Publishers, Inc., 1982.

The Writing and Selling of Fiction, revised, Paul R. Reynolds. New York: William Morrow and Company, Inc., 1980.

The Writing Business, Donald MacCampbell. New York: Crown Publishers, Inc., 1978.

The Writing Business: A Poets & Writers Handbook, by the editors of Coda: Poets & Writers Newsletter. New York: Pushcart Press, 1985.

Writing to Sell, 2nd revised edition, Scott Meredith. New York: Harper & Row, 1977.

Index

About Michael Larsen

Born and educated in New York, Michael Larsen worked in promotion for three major publishers: William Morrow, Bantam, and Pyramid (now Jove). In 1970, he and Elizabeth Pomada, his partner in life and work, moved to San Francisco.

He and Elizabeth started Michael Larsen/Elizabeth Pomada Literary Agents, the Bay Area's oldest literary agency, in 1972. Since then, the agency has sold books mostly by new writers to more than sixty publishers and has had two bestsellers.

Michael lectures on writing, agenting, and publishing and presents workshops based on his book *How to Write a Book Proposal* and a seminar, "The Writer as Warrior: The 100% Solution to Becoming a Successful Author," based on the material in this book, for universities, writers' groups, and writers' conferences. With Hal Zina Bennett he wrote *How to Work with a Collaborator* (published in Spring, 1988).

He has reviewed books for the *San Francisco Chronicle* and his articles have appeared in the *San Francisco Examiner, Writer's Connection, Writer's Digest,* and *Publisher's Weekly.* He conceived and collaborated with Elizabeth on *California Publicity Outlets* (now *Metro California Media*) and *Painted Ladies: San Francisco's Resplendent Victorians,* now in its twelfth printing with 115,000 copies in print. He and Elizabeth have done a sequel to *Painted Ladies* about Victorian houses around the country; *Daughters of Painted Ladies: America's Resplendent Victorians.*

To help maintain his rhythm, he plays drums in a dance band.

OTHER BOOKS IN THE
WRITER'S BASIC BOOKSHELF
SERIES

A Beginner's Guide to Getting Published, edited by Kirk Polking, $10.95

How to Bulletproof Your Manuscript, by Bruce B. Henderson, $9.95

How to Sell & Re-Sell Your Writing, by Duane Newcomb, $11.95

How to Understand & Negotiate a Book Contract or Magazine Agreement, by Richard Balkin, $11.95

How to Write & Sell Column, by Julie Raskin & Carolyn Males, $10.95

How to Write a Book Proposal, by Michael Larsen, $9.95

Literary Agents: How to Get & Work with the Right One for You, by Michael Larsen, $9.95

Professional Etiquette for Writers, by William Brohaugh, $9.95

The 29 Most Common Writing Mistakes & How to Avoid Them, by Judy Delton, $9.95

A Writer's Guide to Research, by Lois Horowitz, $9.95

(For a complete catalog of Writer's Digest Books, write to the address below or call TOLL-FREE 1-800-543-4644, outside Ohio.)

To order directly from the publisher, include $2.00 postage and handling for one book, 50¢ for each additional book. Allow 30 days for delivery. Send to:

Writer's Digest Books
1507 Dana Avenue
Cincinnati, OH 45207

Prices subject to change without notice.